CONSTITUTIONAL REFORM
AND THE FUTURE OF
THE REPUBLIC OF CHINA

Studies of the East Asian Institute—Columbia University

TAIWAN IN THE MODERN WORLD

TAIWAN IN THE MODERN WORLD

CONSTITUTIONAL REFORM AND THE FUTURE OF THE REPUBLIC OF CHINA

Joseph Bosco
Chang Chün-hung
Parris Chang
Cheng Hsing-ti
Antonio Chiang
Chin Sheng-pao
Hungdah Chiu
Chu Yun-han
David Dean
Harvey J. Feldman
Hong Yuh-Chin

Paul S.P. Hsu
Jason C. Hu
Ying-mao Kau
Andrew J. Nathan
Chi Schive
Chi Su
Hung-mao Tien
Tsai Shih-yuan
N.T. Wang
Edwin A. Winckler
Yao Chia-wen

HARVEY J. FELDMAN, EDITOR

An East Gate Book

M. E. Sharpe, Inc.
Armonk, New York
London, England

An East Gate Book

Library of Congress Cataloging-in-Publication Data

Constitutional reform and the future of the Republic of China / edited by
    Harvey J. Feldman.
        p. cm.—(Taiwan in the modern world)
    Papers from the Conference on Constitutional Reform and the Future of the ROC
held Oct. 16–17, 1990 at Columbia University and sponsored by the Taiwan Area
Studies Program of the East Asian Institute, Columbia University.
    Includes index.
    ISBN 0-87332-880-9
    1. Taiwan—Politics and government—1988– —Congresses. 2. Taiwan—
Constitutional history—Congresses. 3. Taiwan—Economic conditions—
1975– —Congresses. I. Feldman, Harvey, 1931– . II. Conference on
Constitutional Reform and the Future of the ROC (1990: Columbia University)
III. Columbia University. Taiwan Area Studies Program. IV. Series.
JQ1521.A2C66   1991
951.249′058—dc20   91-16193
                                                                  CIP

Printed in the United States of America

MV   10   9   8   7   6   5   4   3   2   1

Contents

List of Abbreviations

ADB	Asian Development Bank
DPP	Democratic Progressive Party
GATT	General Agreement on Tariffs and Trade
IGO	International Governmental Organization
IMF	International Monetary Fund
KMT	Kuomintang
NAC	National Affairs Conference
NSC	National Security Council
OECD	Organization for Economic Cooperation and Development
OECDF	Overseas Economic Cooperation and Development Fund
PECC	Pacific Economic Coordination Council
PRC	People's Republic of China
ROC	Republic of China
TASP	Taiwan Area Studies Program, Columbia University
TPKM	Taiwan, Penghu, Kinmen, and Matsu

Foreword

The Taiwan Area Studies Program (TASP) in Columbia University's East Asian Institute was initiated in July 1989, with a grant from the Institute of International Relations of National Chengchi University. Its purpose is to encourage research and teaching on Taiwan at Columbia, and to serve local, national, and international audiences with information on Taiwan provided through conferences, publications, and other programs.

Taiwan's economic achievements, its pathbreaking experiments with political reform, its unique patterns of political participation, its example as a fully modernized Chinese cultural community, its importance in the world trading system, and its key role in Pacific Basin international relations have all made Taiwan the focus of intense interest among students of economic development, comparative politics, and international relations.

Events in Taiwan are fast-moving and complex. They would be difficult to follow from abroad even with adequate press coverage, and are even more elusive without it. The important developments that occurred during and after the National Affairs Conference (NAC) of July 1990 were understood by few Americans, even those who try to keep up with events in Taiwan. TASP decided it was important to bring up-to-date, in-depth information about the NAC before our audience to enable them to analyze the meaning of these events for Taiwan's development. The Conference on Constitutional Reform and the Future of the ROC was held on October 16 and 17, 1990.

Ambassador Harvey Feldman, a member of our program's Advisory Committee, organized this meeting of leading NAC participants and observers. Participants included political figures from both the ruling Kuomintang and the opposition Democratic Progressive Party, and leading scholars from Taiwan and the United States. Many of the speakers, both politicians and scholars, were NAC participants and could report as both eyewitnesses and analysts. The conference unfolded in a lively, informal atmosphere in which participants offered a mixture of information, analysis, and opinion, enabling members of the audience to form their own impressions of the trend of events at a time when it is too early for scholars to draw academic conclusions. We now offer the edited transcript of the proceedings so that a wider audience of readers can do the same.

The Taiwan Area Studies Program is grateful to the Institute of International Relations, National Chengchi University, for its financial support; to Ambassador Feldman for organizing the conference; and to those participants who traveled from afar to share their insights with us. These proceedings offer not only valuable information, but rare insight into the dynamics of political change in Taiwan today.

Andrew J. Nathan
Director
Taiwan Area Studies Program

Preface

The essays and dialogues that follow were initially delivered at a conference that bears the same name as this volume, "Constitutional Reform and the Future of the Republic of China," convoked at Columbia University by the Taiwan Area Studies Program, October 16–17, 1990. The conference planners—Professor Andrew J. Nathan, Dr. Joseph Bosco, and I—began working on the program shortly after President Lee Teng-hui called for an extraordinary National Affairs Conference to be held in Taipei at the end of June. Our intention was to bring to audiences in the United States the key accomplishments of the NAC to discuss how they would affect the politics, economics, and society of the ROC in the decade of the 1990s.

Since the NAC would bring together politicians, academics, professionals, businessmen, including members of the Kuomintang (KMT), the opposition Democratic Progressive Party (DPP), and independents, we hoped to do the same. In fact, we hoped that most of our participants would be people who earlier had taken part in the NAC itself. In this we were reasonably successful: ten of our twenty speakers in fact had been participants in the NAC. Alas, we were somewhat less successful in striking the exact balance we had hoped for between KMT and DPP members since we had one more spokesperson from the opposition than from the ruling party—four to three.

Human history is not a linear progression and neither is the path of democracy. Any expectation of even, steady, unbroken movement from an authoritarian system to one in which democratic practices are firmly institutionalized is entirely too Pollyanna-like. There were halts and stumbles on the way in nineteenth-century America and doubtless that will be true in the ROC. But I think we may say on the basis of developments both before and since the NAC that Taiwan is well and truly embarked on that path, and, barring some entirely unlooked for catastrophe, will continue on it. For that, all its friends and admirers may be thankful.

A word about orthography. As all in the field know, there are umpteen different ways of spelling Chinese terms, particularly personal and place names. In turning oral presentations into written essays, we have used the Wade-Giles system for everything except the names of the paper presenters. For those, we have used the spellings they themselves prefer. This makes for a lack of uniformity, but in things as personal as names, neatness does not count.

Harvey J. Feldman
U.S. Ambassador, retired

Contributors

Joseph Bosco is Associate Director of the Taiwan Area Studies Program and Post-Doctoral Research Scholar at Columbia University's East Asian Institute.

Chang Chün-hung is Secretary-General of the Democratic Progressive Party (DPP), and was a member of the National Affairs Council (NAC).

Parris Chang is Director of the Center for East Asian Studies and Professor of Political Science at Pennsylvania State University. He was a member of the NAC.

Cheng Hsing-ti was born in the Pescadores, an offshore island of Taiwan. He earned his Ph.D. in political science from Southern Illinois University. He is Professor of public policy and research methodology at National Chengchi University and the Deputy Director of the Kuomintang (KMT) Department of Social Affairs.

Antonio Chiang is Editor-in-Chief of *The Journalist Weekly*.

Chin Sheng-pao holds an M.A. from the University of London and is Associate Professor at the Institute of Diplomacy, National Chengchi University. He was a member of the NAC. His most recent publication is *East Asia and the United States in the 1990s* (1991).

Hungdah Chiu is Professor, University of Maryland School of Law, and was a member of the NAC.

Chu Yun-han is Visiting Associate Professor of Political Science, Columbia University, and Associate Professor in the

Department of Political Science, National Taiwan University. He was invited but declined to participate in the NAC.

David Dean is the former Director of the American Institute in Taiwan.

Harvey J. Feldman is a retired diplomat with years of experience in Taiwan. He co-edited *Taiwan in a Time of Transition* (1988).

Hong Yuh-Chin has a doctoral degree in law from Chinese Culture University. He has been a member of the Legislative Yuan (KMT-Tainan County) since 1980, and is the Deputy Director-General of the Policy Coordination Commission of the Kuomintang Central Committee responsible for liaison with opposition parties. He was a member of the NAC.

Paul S.P. Hsu is Professor of Law at National Taiwan University, and a Senior Partner of Lee & Li, Attorneys-at-Law.

Jason C. Hu is Deputy Director of the Sun Yat-sen Center for Policy Studies, National Sun Yat-sen University, and was a member of the NAC.

Ying-mao Kau is Professor of Political Science at Brown University. His scholarly works focus on East Asian politics and international relations. His most recent book is *Moving Toward the 21st Century* (in Chinese). He was a member of the NAC.

Andrew J. Nathan is Professor of Political Science and Director of the Taiwan Area Studies Program, East Asian Institute, Columbia University. His most recent book is *China's Crisis* (1990).

Chi Schive is Professor of Economics in the Department and Graduate Institute of Economics, College of Law, National Taiwan University. He is the author of *The Foreign Factor: The Multinational Corporation's Contribution to the Economic Modernization of the Republic of China* (1990).

Chi Su received a Ph.D. in political science from Columbia University, as well as a certificate from Columbia's Harriman Institute (formerly Russian Institute). He is currently Deputy Director of the Institute of International Relations, National Chengchi University, and Professor in the Department of Diplomacy. He has written on Sino-Soviet-American relations and the ROC's foreign policy. His latest publication is *The Sino-Soviet Normalization Process: 1979–1989* (1990).

Hung-mao Tien is Professor of Political Science at the University of Wisconsin-Milwaukee. He is author of *The Great Transition: Political and Social Change in the Republic of China* (1989) and was a member of the NAC.

Tsai Shih-yuan is a National Assemblyman (DPP–Taipei) and a Visiting Scholar at Harvard Law School (1990–91). He has a Ph.D. in psychology from American University. For the past decade he has been active in Taiwanese politics and has held various posts, including Publisher of *Progress Magazine* (1983–86), Chairman of the Central Advisory Committee of the DPP (1987–88), and Deputy Secretary-General of the DPP (1988–90).

N.T. Wang is Director of the China-International Business Project, Adjunct Professor in the Columbia University Graduate School of Business and School of International and Public Affairs, and a Senior Research Associate at the East Asian Institute. He is the author (with Teng Weizao) of *Transnational*

Corporations and China's Open Door Policy (1988), and editor of *Taiwan Enterprises in Global Perspective* (forthcoming).

Edwin A. Winckler is a Research Associate at the East Asian Institute, Columbia University. He is editor (with Susan Greenhalgh) of *Contending Approaches to the Political Economy of Taiwan* (1988).

Yao Chia-wen is a member of the DPP Standing Committee, an attorney, and was a member of the NAC.

CONSTITUTIONAL REFORM
AND THE FUTURE OF
THE REPUBLIC OF CHINA

The Constitutional Conundrum
and the Need for Reform

Harvey J. Feldman
We obviously are at a very interesting time in Taiwan's political and economic development. As someone who has been studying the Republic of China on Taiwan for a number of years, I would say it used to be easy. In the past nothing happened very quickly. You had time to wrap your mind around events in Taiwan because evolution proceeded at a slow, at times it seemed a glacial pace. But that's not the case any more. Now events crowd us very rapidly. The last few years have seen remarkable developments happening with remarkable speed. Most recently we've had the National Affairs Conference (NAC). This was part of an on-rushing pattern of political changes, which are having the effect of amending the constitution of the Republic of China, just as the constitution was effectively amended by the adoption of the Temporary Provisions back in 1948. The disappearance of the Temporary Provisions over the next year in effect will re-amend the constitutional arrangements of the Republic of China.

We want to talk about these things. We want to understand the evolution that's taking place now. And we want to put it in the context of the 1990s and beyond. It's a cliché of the last several months to say that we now live in the post–Cold War era. But cliché or not, it's true. This will mean, inevitably, massive changes in the world, and one hopes in the way our government responds to the world.

It was clear to me as a practitioner of policy in the State Department that the United States for long years had no Taiwan policy at all. Policy toward the Republic of China was simply an adjunct of our policy toward mainland China. In the days when the PRC was the red demon of Asia, we wrapped ourselves around Taiwan in response. We concluded the Mutual Defense Treaty, provided military assistance, economic assistance, and so on. At a time when the administrations in Washington saw the government in Beijing as a possible counterweight to the Soviet Union in the worldwide struggle of the two superpowers, Taiwan was seen as an embarrassment to the growing relations with the PRC. But if there is no longer a superpower confrontation, if the Cold War is indeed over as NATO and President Bush have proclaimed, then to use a memorable phrase coined by Harry Harding, perhaps we will see mainland China looming smaller on the international scene. And perhaps over this decade, the decade of the 1990s, the United States will really for the first time adopt a Taiwan policy. That, if it happens, will happen not just because of what happens in Washington, but because of what happens in Taipei, and this is what we want to explore over these next two days.

We will begin by looking at the constitutional situation of the Republic of China and the need for reform.

Hung-mao Tien
Constitutional reform in the Republic of China on Taiwan must be looked at from the standpoint of the political transformation that is taking place. The political system on Taiwan has long been marked by one party authoritarianism. The system now is on the way to some kind of democratic transition. The transition raises many important questions for comparative politics. There are few other political systems where the ruling party is as thoroughly in charge as in the Republic of China. Taiwan's Kuomintang in many respects resembles a Leninist party, although there are also several different features. Given that situation, the transition to democracy is even more difficult. One of the most important obstacles for democratic transition is the constitutional question. The issues at stake in part reflect the historical legacy of the KMT, and also the continuing political

rivalry between Taiwan and mainland China.

Shortly after the adoption of the 1947 constitution, the National Assembly adopted the so-called Temporary Provisions of 1948. They were a series of articles attached to the original body of the constitution, added because China was in the midst of civil war. It was thought that some of the constitutional articles adopted a year before needed to be temporarily suspended, the president needed to be given extraordinary powers, and some kind of additional institution had to be created in order to deal with the emergencies derived from the civil war.

After moving to Taiwan, in 1954 the ROC regime through its National Assembly extended the period of effectiveness of the Temporary Provisions. Since then, there have been four major revisions. Each time new articles were added which in the eyes of many people further revised the content of the original constitution. But now many people on the island believe that the emergencies that provided the justification for adoption of the Temporary Provisions no longer exist, and that many of these articles conflict with the constitution itself. They point to the suspension of civil rights that are protected in the constitution, the extraordinary power given to the president, and the existence of several institutions, such as Garrison Command and the National Security Council, created under the Temporary Provisions that they believe should either be abolished or substantially revised.

Constitutional reform has become a matter of urgency in Taiwan because many national institutions that have existed for forty years are no longer functioning properly. The most important institutional question concerns the national representative bodies: the National Assembly, which has the power to elect the president and the vice-president and to amend and revise the constitution; the Legislative Yuan, comparable to the parliament in parliamentary democracies; and the Control

Yuan, which exercises supervision over the conduct of public officials. As they exist today, they have a majority of members elected on the mainland in the late 1940s. In the National Assembly, 630 members were elected in the mainland in the 1940s or added to the body in the last forty years in a manner not subject to election. Only 80 of the 700 members were elected in the area under the Republic of China's current jurisdiction. In the Legislative Yuan of 270 members, 140 were elected in the 1940s. Only 130 were elected in Taiwan or from the overseas Chinese community. In the Control Yuan of 51 members, 20 were elected in the 1940s, and only 31 were elected from the Taiwan area.

The Council of Grand Justices recently ruled that all of the members elected on the mainland must retire by the end of 1991. This appears to have temporarily resolved some of the questions concerning the national representative bodies. But the question of the composition and the methods of electing members of these bodies remains highly controversial in light of the fact that the government has decided to include among these members a certain percentage of delegates who will continue to represent mainland constituencies.

A second important institutional issue is whether Taiwan should have a presidential system, a parliamentary democracy, or some combination of the two. Many scholars argue that the constitution provides for a political system like the parliamentary democracies of Western Europe, though this is not beyond dispute. In any case, the Temporary Provisions gave tremendous power to the presidency. In the last forty years the system in fact became a presidential system, concentrating major power in the hands of a president who simultaneously filled the position of leader of the ruling KMT.

A final issue in the constitutional debate has been raised by the opposition party, the Democratic Progressive Party (DPP), which has called for adopting a totally new constitution, rather than simply revising the 1947 constitution or abolishing the Temporary Provisions. They raise fundamental questions of the sovereignty and jurisdiction of the Republic of China: Is Taiwan to be part of China or does the government have jurisdiction and sovereignty over Taiwan alone? Mainlander old guards and other KMT conservatives believe that adopting a new constitution is virtual declaration of Taiwan as a new independent state. If successful, there would no longer be a Republic of China. They are emotionally opposed to a new constitution. Thus opinions regarding constitutional reform are highly polarized.

Hong Yuh-Chin

The Constitution of the Republic of China was written to apply to the whole of China. Yet today the constitution can only be applied in the province of Taiwan. According to the constitution, the Legislative Yuan should enact legislation to implement self-government at the provincial and county levels. But for forty years the ruling power of the central government has applied only to the province of Taiwan. This has led to an as yet unresolved constitutional debate concerning whether the principle of self-government for provinces and counties should be instituted. Under these circumstances, a genuine system of local self-government that coincides with the stipulations of the constitution has yet to appear.

In March 1948, after the constitution went into effect, the first National Assembly met in Nanking. At that time the Chinese Communists were already staging a serious military rebellion. Thus soon after the Sino-Japanese War ended in 1945, the government once again encountered a state of war. Viewing the difficulties of the national situation, the members of the National Assembly decided to invoke the first clause of Article 174, "The Procedure for Revising the Constitution," in order to legislate the "Temporary Provisions in Effect During the Period of Communist Rebellion." This declaration of what amounted to a state of martial law proclaimed that:

> In this Period of Communist Rebellion, for the sake of avoiding the emergent political crisis, and addressing the mammoth economic change, the president is empowered to adopt emergency measures through a resolution of a cabinet meeting of the Executive Yuan. The president's power will not be limited by the regular procedures of Articles 39 and 43 of the constitution.

This extreme measure was taken in order to empower the president with capabilities to respond to the vast challenges in this troubled period.

Initially, most people expected the Period of Communist Rebellion to end within three years. Yet, unfortunately, owing to the continuing tense situation in the Taiwan Straits, it has lasted much longer. Although our constitution has been in effect for more than forty-three years, this suspension of some of its provisions can no longer be called "temporary."

Since the Temporary Provisions have been in effect, their scope and powers have been revised and expanded four times, causing the Temporary Provisions to deviate seriously from the spirit of constitutionalism. These provisions, seen by many as an illegal twisting of the constitution, were seriously criticized after the period of strong-man rule ended, opening up the Taiwan political arena considerably.

The essential points of this critique are as follows:

(1) The constitution merely grants the National Assembly the power to revise it; it has never authorized the power to legislate any kind of Temporary Provisions.

(2) The enactment of the Temporary Provisions is the kind of conduct that undermines the constitution—even if it is legal, it should be avoided at all costs.

(3) Numerous clauses in the Temporary Provisions were written for the strong men's specific needs. Hence they should

be discarded now that this era has passed.
The above criticisms of the Temporary Provisions certainly have
both a theoretical and a practical basis that are especially
pertinent now, since everyone is demanding that the government
quickly end the authoritarian system characteristic of the Period
of Communist Rebellion.

Nonetheless, we should not entirely deny the contribution of
the Temporary Provisions to certain stages of the history of the
ROC. For example, I remember that in the 1970s the Temporary
Provisions were revised in the year following the ROC's
withdrawal from the United Nations. Other opportune revisions
involved the measure for supplementary elections, adopted in
1966, and the measure to increase the number of
parliamentarians from the Free Region (clause no. 6 of the
Temporary Provisions), which posed for a time a conflict
between the operations of democratic politics and the goal of
unification.

Moreover, the original shortcomings of the constitution itself
are one historical factor adding to the present problems of the
constitutional government. When the constitution was first put
into effect, on one hand, it did not continue the spirit of the draft
constitution of May 5, 1946, which was superior in design to the
final document; on the other hand, the negotiations between all
political parties and factions caused the text of the constitution to
be affected by the shadow of political compromise. For example,
the difference between the rights and powers of the president and
those of the premier were not made clear, thus easily leading to
an unstable political process.

(In my opinion, the system of the Temporary Provisions gave
the president powers akin to those of an emperor—hence the
above comment about the instability of the political process is a
moot point.)

Another important area where the constitution is lacking is the
problem of the relations among the five yuan.

(1) The functions and powers of the Legislative Yuan and the Control Yuan are not made totally clear, hence these two bodies are sometimes in conflict.

(2) The powers of the National Assembly are not well designed. Besides the right to elect and impeach the president and vice-president, it can set legal principles, as well as consider laws passed by the Legislative Yuan. In addition, it holds the power to revise the constitution itself. Yet, if the National Assembly were actually to use those powers it would certainly come into serious conflict with the Legislative Yuan. These fundamental deficiencies of the constitution have been exposed in the past two months in the struggle between the Legislative Yuan and the National Assembly over which has the power to guide the revision of the constitution.

The difficulties of constitutional politics have led to a number of serious consequences. First is the embarrassing situation of the ROC's "long parliament." The true meaning of "parliamentary democratic politics" is to organize a parliament representing all the people through a process whereby citizens regularly elect representatives who embody a pluralistic society. Yet because of the protection given by the Council of Grand Justices in Interpretations No. 31 and No. 6 of the Temporary Provisions, the parliament has not stood for reelection in the past forty years in the ROC—the same parliament that was elected in 1947 is still in session. Unfortunately, most representatives are over eighty years of age and have lost touch with the concerns of the voters in Taiwan. Hence the demand that the whole parliament stand for election is no longer just a political slogan, it is a popular consensus. Not long ago, the Council of Grand Justices announced Interpretation No. 261, which states that the central representatives should all retire by no later than the end of 1991. Hence, this particular constitutional problem should be resolved soon.

Second is the fact that the authoritarian system lives on. The

ROC Constitution mandates a parliamentary system of organization. However, our president is not just a symbolic leader like the queen of England. In order to broaden presidential powers beyond those prescribed in the parliamentary system, the Temporary Provisions were put into effect, granting the president broad emergency powers. As supplemented and revised, they extended the presidential powers even more. Not only has the constitutional system of parliamentary government been dyed with the color of the presidential system, but a situation has evolved where the democratic politics of responsible government has been greatly distorted. As the Chinese saying goes, "One who is of power is without responsibility, while one who is of responsibility is without power."

Since Mr. Lee Teng-hui became president, due to his great intelligence and patience, much progress has been made. He has officially announced several times that he would like to return to the constitutional limit of two presidential terms in office. Moreover, he intends to reduce the importance of the National Security Council—the so-called shadow cabinet which is an organization dating from the Period of Communist Rebellion—by reducing the frequency of its meetings. Since martial law was lifted, all political taboos were lifted as well, reshaping the previous authoritarian system, and making such organizations as the National Security Council largely redundant. Of course, the fundamental undertaking must be to abolish the authoritarian system once and for all—to prevent the strong-man system of government from further eroding the regular constitutional system of the ROC.

Third, local self-government still lacks legitimation. The highest legal basis for the local system of government should be the constitution. However, right now in Taiwan most important regulations concerning local self-government are issued by executive order, instead of by law. This is against the spirit of the constitution. Moreover, for the sake of avoiding elections of the governor of Taiwan and the mayors of Taipei and Kaohsiung—which the opposition party would likely win—the central government has purposely postponed carrying out the legitimation of local self-government operations. This situation caused the process of local self-government in the province of Taiwan for the past forty years to stagnate, staying in the stage of what Sun Yat-sen called a "tutelage" under the guidance of the KMT. This kind of deliberate obstruction makes it difficult to institutionalize a system of constitutional democracy—a situation that must be corrected as soon as possible.

The above considerations show that not only is constitutional reform necessary, but its time frame must be shortened and the scale of reform enlarged. Otherwise we will have no way to satisfy the requirements of the country's political and economic development. By convening the National Affairs Conference, President Lee broke the bonds of the unreasonable structure of the system by appealing to social powers beyond the narrow scope of politics. This conference was also a formal step in his movement toward constitutional reform. In the conference, people from all parties and all socioeconomic levels, coming from the ROC and abroad, gathered together to prescribe a cure for our constitutional conundrum.

In fact, the National Affairs Conference was in many ways a preparatory meeting for further discussions of constitutional reform. In the six days, much ground was covered: all issues raised received quite tangible consideration from all parties. The next step for President Lee is to transform the mutual understanding of the conference into concrete acts of constitutional reform.

In guiding this epic task of reform, President Lee has undertaken a truly difficult and vitally important endeavor. I have every confidence that he can complete this task in the two years he has set as his goal.

In conclusion, one historical barrier to establishing a healthy constitutional system has been the mentality of the ruling party. From its early days in Taiwan, the KMT has had the attitude of being a temporary guest on the island. Another big barrier has been the fantasy of Taiwan independence, recently raised daily by the opposition party. Today in the ROC, constitutional reform involves a process of transformation from the emergency system of the Period of Communist Rebellion to a regular system; likewise, it is also a process of transformation from the era of strong-man rule to constitutional democracy. We should seek a constitutional framework that is flexible enough to be able to adjust to contemporary needs as well as future developments. In my opinion, only under democratic constitutional operations will we be able to begin to relieve the crisis of national identity and the debate between re-unification and independence.

Actually, during the seven presidential terms of office that have passed since the constitution was promulgated, the presidents have seldom fulfilled their responsibilities of executing the constitution. No doubt certain factors limited their ability to fulfill these responsibilities. However, today objective circumstances no longer allow the government to postpone or avoid the operation of the constitution. On the contrary, now we enjoy the most beneficial social conditions under which we can reform our constitution. How to enrich the "Taiwan economic miracle" with a democratic component is something all people should carefully consider—people from all political parties as well as scholars and experts. Let us then roll up our sleeves and figure out the best way out of our constitutional conundrum.

Edwin A. Winckler
With so many distinguished scholars and politicians from Taiwan here, it is useless for a foreigner living in New York City to talk about the details of recent political developments on Taiwan. Instead I will raise some questions about those developments by drawing on recent comparative literature about political

transition. There is a general question I want to address, both today and tomorrow: "Is this political miracle half full or half empty?" My answer is "just about." That is, in 1990, Taiwan is about halfway through its political transition, in a truly transitional "twilight zone" that is neither authoritarianism nor democracy. The only way I can think of approaching Taiwan's current situation is to look backward to the authoritarian system from which we have come, which is what I will do today, and forward to some kind of democratic system that we can posit, which is what I'll do tomorrow. Unfortunately, comparative "transition theory" is in about the same condition: the literature on the transition "from authoritarianism" is more developed than the literature on the transition "to democracy."

Today I will start with some comments on the state of "discourse" about transition and Taiwan. Then I will briefly discuss what kind of an authoritarian system Taiwan used to be. After that I will note three characteristics of Taiwan's transition "from authoritarianism" that the comparative literature suggests. Basically, I am impressed with the performance of both the KMT and DPP. As I will elaborate tomorrow, I'm also rather optimistic about Taiwan's political future. However, today I'm going to take a pessimistic, critical approach, viewing the glass as half empty rather than half full.

As regards discourse, in the late 1980s Harvey Feldman was timely in editing a book called *Taiwan in a Time of Transition*. Now in the early 1990s he has again been timely with his focus on constitutionalism. So, both today and tomorrow, I will devote some attention to its role in transitions, on Taiwan in particular. It is tiresome of academics to raise definitional questions, but discourse about democracy is problematic in any language. It is even more problematic when one must translate concepts back and forth between English and Chinese. The Western tradition contains at least three fundamentally different conceptions of constitutionalism, which

I will label conservative, radical, and liberal.

The oldest and best statement is the ancient one of Aristotle: the constitution of a country is "what constitutes" the country, a summary that "conserves" its historical and social essence. That's an extremely comprehensive definition but, for many purposes, the most workable one. It should appeal to most Chinese, who know that politics is too complicated for easy summary.

The main modern Western concept, from continental Europe, is radical: A constitution is a document that prescribes how to abolish an undesirable historically-inherited political system and how to construct an ideal modern political one. This definition appeals to Third World reformers attempting to overcome traditionalism, imperialism, or authoritarianism. It was the hope of twentieth-century Chinese constitutionalists, particularly those who favored parliamentarism, during the drafting of the 1947 Chinese constitution, and during the current attempt on Taiwan to revive it. The reformist idealism of this radical approach is perhaps reflected in the fact that Taiwan's parliamentarists continue to insist that the 1947 constitution is basically parliamentary. In fact, even the document itself was a mixed parliamentary and president system and, as implemented, it was basically presidential, not to say pseudo-Leninist and authoritarian. Incidentally, Aristotle argued that mixed systems are more stable than monistic ones, so Taiwan should probably be reassured that its constitution is a hodgepodge, not worried by it.

The third definition of a constitution, the liberal one, is a compromise between the first two. It is the Madisonian deployment of checks and balances to occupy the feasible middle ground between the historically real and the politically ideal. It attempts to design institutions that will keep politicians from murdering each other, and keep the state from oppressing society. I assume that's what Taiwan is groping toward, but I do not assume that the American system, or any other, is an adequate model that Taiwan can copy. On the contrary, Americans have their own problems in reconciling ideals and reality.

As regards the transition "from authoritarianism" on Taiwan, we must clarify from what kind of authoritarianism Taiwan is starting. The most common notion is that Taiwan has been some kind of party system. This is partly a journalistic habit—the Nationalist party did this, the Nationalist party did that. We've heard that for forty years, mostly because the Nationalist party has claimed to be the "ruling party." (That's a phrase that must be consigned to the dustbin of history as quickly as possible, if democratization is to proceed. It makes the KMT sound like an emperor that is going to rule forever. Taiwan needs a different term for "incumbent" party, to emphasize the democratic possibility of alternation in power with the "opposition.")

Viewing Taiwan as a party system is also a habit of academics. This was true in the past, for both sinologists and comparativists, even those who knew something about Taiwan. Most academics read only the journalists, and most of the rest listened only to the Nationalists. Diplomats—Kerr, Whiting, Clough, Feldman, Pratt—did much better. Now we have a new wave of academics, most of whom never paid attention to Taiwan before, but who are now repelled by the PRC's repression of political-economic progress, or attracted by Taiwan's new funding for research about Taiwan. They can't be bothered to find out much about the place, but want to publish rapidly on the subject, so they find it convenient to think of Taiwan as a Leninist party system in transition to a competitive party system. That way they can reduce Taiwan to categories they think they already understand. Unfortunately it is pretty unclear what a Leninist system is, particularly in the Chinese context. Anyway Taiwan has not been a Leninist political system, partly because the KMT is only partly Leninist, but mostly because Taiwan's political system has been only partly partyist. For both political control of the state and for political penetration of society, the KMT has been only one institution among several, and not as fundamental as the KMT has pretended.

The second major image of Taiwan's political system, recently in academia, is the developmentalist state. This directs attention to the government, to the role of technocrats in policy formulation, and to the role of the state in economic development. This is important to "statists" debunking the role of the market. They are correct to reject a liberal economic interpretation, but wrong to assume that the Nationalist state was as responsible for Taiwan's economic accomplishments as it claims. In any case, though the government technocracy is important to economic policy, it is not so important for political reform.

If authoritarian Taiwan was fundamentally neither a Leninist party nor a developmentalist state, what was it? In plain English, a military dictatorship. Of course, this is not technically adequate—Alfred Stepan has explained many distinctions necessary for discussing the possible roles of the military in politics. Nevertheless, "military dictatorship" is a conveniently loose phrase. It allows us to say that Taiwan is in transition from having been mostly "dictatorship" to being merely "military."

Chiang Kai-shek, who built the old system, was a dictator who used the military as his main base, decorated it with a party, and made the government serve the military. Chiang Ching-kuo, who inherited the old system, also was a dictator, though his original power base lay more in the internal than the external security apparatus. Lee Teng-hui is not a dictator, which leads political journalists on Taiwan to declare the end of "strong-man rule." That's the main point but not the whole story. Dictatorship was not just a personal characteristic of

Chiang Kai-shek and Chiang Ching-kuo, but the institutional core of Nationalist authoritarianism. As Mark Pratt has argued, by preventing a strong man from emerging as his successor, Chiang Ching-kuo probably intended to force the Nationalist state toward more pluralism. Nevertheless, for the moment what Taiwan has is a strong-man system without a strong man.

The political system is still grounded in the security apparatus, internal and external, and that apparatus still sets the basic parameters for politics. Thus, in the middle of the National Affairs Conference, KMT Secretary-General James Soong told the DPP leadership, "You know, the military won't stand for this, we have to cool it." Or in the middle of a recent DPP conference, he summoned the DPP leadership and said, "You've got to change that resolution because Premier Hau is convening the security agencies to put you in jail." There you see exposed the bedrock of Taiwan's political system, more fundamental than whether Taiwan is a presidential or parliamentary system. As in the South American and Southern European transitions, the basic problem remains reducing the role of the military.

As regards Taiwan's transition "from authoritarianism," in comparative perspective three main things are distinctive. First is the gradualism of the process. Gradualism has many advantages—little political violence, little economic disruption, little sociocultural antagonism. However, it also has disadvantages. Transition is constantly in danger of being arrested and reversed. The authoritarian state has not collapsed or been overthrown. It's still there and you have to keep negotiating with it and prodding it to move forward. Particularly in the case of Taiwan, which ostensibly already has a civilian regime, there has been no clear "military moment" in the transition process when Taiwan got rid of the military and its influence. As a result, the military presence continues to haunt the process long after the military issue was resolved in the successful Latin American or Southern European transitions.

Since it's hidden, it's hard to eradicate. Which is the way smart power holders, like senators in Washington, like to exercise power anyway.

From this point of view, President Lee's selection of General Hau as premier is very profound. Whether it turns out to be profoundly wise or profoundly stupid only time will tell. At the moment, things don't look too good, because it appears that Hau is running the government instead of Lee. But at least Lee addressed the central issue of Taiwan's political transition, namely how to maintain military support for the process. I must add, only partly in jest, that in Latin America the way the civilians finally got rid of the military was to turn the government over to them. The military discovered that it was no fun running a government and eventually returned it to the civilians. Maybe on Taiwan too General Hau and the military will get exasperated and get out.

A second characteristic of Taiwan's transition is centrism of elites. I am referring to the idea, well known in transition theory but little applied to Taiwan, that political transition involves an interplay between four actors, not two: conservatives and progressives within the establishment, and moderates and radicals within the opposition. What has made Taiwan's transition "from authoritarianism" so successful so far is the ability of Nationalist progressives and opposition moderates to cooperate with each other. It's fascinating to watch the continuing interplay of those four tendencies. However, one should add at least one qualification for Taiwan—this political spectrum is not just horizontal but also vertical. That is, it's not just from extreme right to extreme left, but also from heavy-weights who still control the basic political power to light-weights whose grip on power is precarious.

A third characteristic of Taiwan's transition is the patience of publics. Guillermo O'Donnell and Philippe Schmitter posited what they called the "mobilization cycle." You can't have a political transition without public involvement. One can admire the people of Taiwan for their patience. However, one can also worry whether transition will succeed if the public sits on the sidelines forever. Some people on Taiwan think they've seen a lot of political unrest so far, but actually the mobilization card has been played very sparingly. The threat of disorder was important for initiating political change around 1975, and then provided an excuse for arresting it around 1980. Nevertheless the opposition has never been very successful, in terms of the proportions of the total population, in getting people into the streets. So far the only moment when public mobilization has been decisive was spring 1990 when finally the students, intellectuals, and middle class came out because they were angry at the self-aggrandizing antics of the National Assembly. But even that was a rather small mobilization relative to those in many other transitions. So I would suggest that the mobilization card has barely begun to be played yet, and that it must be held ready, worrisome though it is.

In conclusion, viewing Taiwan's political transitions as "half empty," the real Taiwan political miracle is that this farce is still going on after forty years. The real Taiwan political miracle is that the conservatives still exercise so much influence. The real Taiwan political miracle is the extraordinary civility of civilian elites, including opposition leaders previously incarcerated. The real Taiwan political miracle is not the "wise leadership" of the Nationalist party, but the phenomenal patience of the Taiwanese public. Since of course there are no miracles, these characteristics point to the fundamentally military nature of the system. Otherwise why so many political concessions to the political right? Why so many opposition conversions from radical to moderate? Why such public hesitance to mobilize? If I were "the KMT" or, as I would prefer to say, General Hau and the military, I wouldn't count on that elite civility and public patience lasting much longer.

—Floor Discussion—

The Chairman (Harvey J. Feldman)
Before opening this up for general discussion, I want to summarize some of the ideas we've heard. The basic question is, "What is Taiwan's political system, and what should it be?" Another question that has been raised is, "If the constitution needs to be amended, how can this be accomplished when it is the National Assembly that has to do the amending, a process that will necessarily undercut its own power?" (Because to create a practical, effective, and fair constitutional system many of the people who are now in the National Assembly will have to lose their positions.) We have an interesting and clear discussion of the conflict between constitution and practice in Mr. Hong's presentation. As Ed Winckler points out, the struggle is not so much between the KMT and the DPP, as between factions within the KMT that are struggling against each other, factions within the DPP that are struggling against each other, and coalitions that form, coalesce, and reform. Another question is, "Will the country continue to need a strong man to coordinate between party, military, and government? Or is that system going to change?" And, as Ed Winckler prompts us, "What is the role of the public in this process?" Are they simply spectators? Are they going to sit back and watch it, or are they going to take a hand in the process?

James Seymour (Senior Research Scholar, Columbia University East Asian Institute)
I hope we will keep our minds focused on the question of constitutionalism. The purpose of a constitution is to keep the government honest and accountable—hopefully accountable to the people, if that is what the constitution says. I agree with almost everything that Ed Winckler said, except brushing aside the present constitution. The problem with the present constitution

isn't that it's a bad constitution. It's that it exists only on paper. It's never really been followed. The government has rather casually brushed it aside whenever the constitution was inconvenient.

What has to be done is instill respect for the rule of law and the rule of the constitution. I think the Taiwanese people, with their Japanese background and their sense of rules, have this idea pretty firmly in mind. But the Kuomintang does not. So the question I want to pose is, how are you going to have a constitution that the leaders will feel bound by? If the leaders say, "Well, we don't like this particular clause, we'll just ignore it," you don't really have a constitutional system. Given the precedents of the last few decades, how are you going to prevent abuses of power? How are you going to prevent the leaders saying, "We don't want the public to hear what that particular political leader is saying, so we are going to lock that person up."

I hope there will be discussion during this conference on how to have firm protections of civil liberties, so that the public can gain access to information and ideas that will enable them to make the decisions, rather than having the decisions made for them by manipulative leaders.

Dennis Engbarth (Senior Editor, *Business International*)
My question is for Mr. Hong Yuh-Chin. Given the difficulty of accomplishing constitutional reform through the current National Assembly and the Legislative Yuan, why doesn't Lee Teng-hui simply use the power of the Temporary Provisions to sweep the slate clean of the irrationalities that have been brought into the political process by the Temporary Provisions? He could create a situation where you start over, call for new elections, get the process rolling on a level at which some of these contradictions from the historical past can simply be discarded.

Hong Yuh-Chin

I think I have addressed your questions in my report. As for the emergency powers given to the president under the Temporary Provisions, President Lee has shown great self-restraint and has declared many times that his term of office will coincide with what the constitution requires, that is, that the president can only be re-elected once. He also downgraded the importance of the National Security Council, so the NSC does not meet often. President Lee is determined to restore constitutional democracy. If President Lee used the powers from Temporary Provisions to solve the conflicts between the National Assembly and the Legislative Yuan, I think this method would contradict the president's original goal of restoring constitutional democracy. Thus we had better use constitutional reforms to solve the conflicts between the National Assembly and the Legislative Yuan.

Hung-mao Tien

His question is about whether the president should use the emergency powers to end the term of old legislators.

Hong Yuh-Chin

Reform doesn't need revolutionary means. Although the president has emergency powers, he has shown self-restraint. The Judicial Yuan explained this clearly in Opinion No. 261. All members of the National Assembly and the Legislative Yuan will retire at the end of 1991. In the near future we will solve this problem. We have already waited for forty years, why can't we wait one more year?

The National Affairs Conference:
Its Meaning and Results

Jason C. Hu

It is a great pleasure to be here and to talk to you about the National Affairs Conference. It was a privilege to be part of that conference. I must make it clear that what I'm going to say is purely my individual opinion and observations. I do not seek to represent the KMT. I have not been briefed about any line I should follow, nor have I been authorized by anybody to speak for them. I aim to present an eyewitness account of what happened in the NAC.

The impetus for the conference was provided by what might be called the "Taipei Spring": the student demonstration in front of the Chiang Kai-shek Memorial Hall in March 1990. Yet many people, the KMT, and the government thought that convening a conference as early as July or even later would be premature. The president of the Judicial Yuan, Lin Yang-kang, said two weeks ago that he still thought the National Affairs Conference had been convened prematurely.

I was personally involved in and would like to share with you some of the panel discussions in preparation for the National Affairs Conference. The NAC secretariat convened more than twelve sessions of informal discussions between the Preparatory Committee and groups of academics or journalists, each time involving more than ten people. In my session there were twelve political science and law professors. In that meeting, which took place at the end of May, I suggested what I called the Five-No Principles.

First, the conference should not try to solve everything in one attempt. We should not involve constitutional reform and mainland policy in a single conference. We could have one conference on constitutional reform in July and have another one on mainland questions in December, so as to solve problems more easily and keep everybody cool and calm. Second, I said that the secretariat should prepare study papers before the conference started. Otherwise people would go into the conference and start talking without preparation, and we would achieve nothing. Third, the conference should serve the purpose of political communication, and should not necessarily seek a consensus. The majority should not force the minority to a conclusion that they are not willing to uphold. Fourth, I suggested that we should not allow the National Affairs Conference to be a media show. In Taiwan, whenever you turn a TV camera on, people get excited, and they sometimes engage in "extra-curricular activities," that is, physical violence. Fifth, I said this should not be a party-to-party struggle. The conference should be a voluntary forum for all people who want to contribute their wisdom and ideas for the reform of the country.

My Five-No policy of course was not adopted in full by the secretariat. Some points were adopted. My suggestion for two conferences instead of one was never adopted. Some of the issues remained contested up to the eve of the conference. The DPP wanted it to become a party-to-party affair. The KMT resisted that. Some people insisted that the agreements or resolutions of the conference must have binding force on the government. The government did not accept this.

Some people said that the conference must have conclusions or even resolutions adopted by vote. Others argued that even if we did vote, the resolution would not have binding effect, and that voting was therefore pointless. In the end, polls were taken by show of hands to indicate impressions and wishes, but no votes were taken.

Consensus was reached on many points, but I will outline only the seven most important of them. The most important of all was on the question of mainland policy. It was agreed, I think, by all participants that no policy should be adopted that would jeopardize the security or well-being of the twenty million residents of Taiwan. Whether the policy be unification or independence, it should not jeopardize or damage the well-being and security of the people of Taiwan. The conference was in complete consensus on this issue.

The second consensus was that the ROC should abolish the Temporary Provisions. The third consensus was a feeling that the political system in Taiwan should be changed by constitutional revision instead of by adopting a new constitution. One day an opinion poll was taken at the conference. Of 131 persons present, 93 of them, about 71 percent, said that the constitution should be revised instead of replaced by a new constitution. Those saying a new constitution was needed were 32 persons, about 24 percent, of whom only 9 percent were for what we call the "Great Democratic Constitution" or "Democratic Magna Carta." Among others, only 5 persons were for a Basic Law to replace our existing constitution temporarily until national reunification is achieved. Interestingly, advocates of the Great Democratic Constitution and the Basic Law have quieted down since the end of the NAC and now focus on the effort for constitutional revision. This is a reflection of true democratic spirit.

Fourth, in keeping with the principle of changing but not abolishing the present political system, the general tendency of the conference was to maintain the present five-powers system, although there were people who strongly advocated a unicameral system, and some who said that the Control Yuan or the Examination Yuan should be abolished. A fifth consensus was that the senior parliamentarians in the National Assembly, Control Yuan, and Legislative Yuan must all retire as soon as possible, no later than December 31, 1991. Sixth, the majority of the participants in the conference showed a willingness to accept the proportional representation system in a new or revised parliamentary body, as a way of selecting "National Representatives at Large." They would replace the current overseas Chinese representatives, women's representatives, professional representatives, and might also serve to represent the mainland constituencies.

Seventh, there was a general agreement on the direct election of the governor of Taiwan and mayors of the two special municipalities (Taipei and Kaohsiung), and that this should be done as soon as possible. "The earlier the better" was the phrase used in the conference, but certainly by the end of 1991, the same time that the new parliament should be elected.

There were three key points on which we did not reach consensus. The first one was whether to elect the president directly or indirectly. The media in Taiwan reported at one juncture that it was a consensus of the conference to have a direct election of the president. But I must say this was not true in reality. Second, we did not reach a consensus on the procedures for revising the constitution, whether it should go through the Legislative Yuan or through the National Assembly. I think the majority was in favor of the Legislative Yuan doing the revision, and then sending it to the National Assembly for adoption. The last point I think we did not really agree upon was how to make sure that the conclusions or consensuses of the National Affairs Conference would be honored and implemented by the government. This was not clearly spelled out in the conclusions of the conference.

I felt personally that the National Affairs Conference was a positive and encouraging development. During and after the conference, people like us were bombarded by telephone calls asking, "How could you let dissidents like so-and-so and so be allowed into the National Affairs Conference?" "How could you let previous political prisoners be guests of the president?" "How could you let deviant political positions like independence be aired publicly on television, in radio, in the papers?" A lot of people were not prepared to accept a more open and democratic political atmosphere. I went on television once to say that if we are going toward further democratization, this is a process we have to go through. You have to get used to this in a democratic society. You have to hear the political points of view that you don't enjoy, or agree with. This in itself is an encouraging development and an educational experience for the people in Taiwan.

I was very impressed with the friendly atmosphere of the National Affairs Conference. There were arguments, but I had been concerned that a conference participated in by our good friends from the DPP might turn out to be a forum with some physical actions like seizing the microphone or throwing chairs. None of that happened. It was held in a truly democratic and friendly atmosphere, and showed that both the KMT and the DPP were not monsters, were reasonable human beings, and that they and the DPP could learn to work with each other.

Many people feel that the government has not done enough to implement the conclusions of the National Affairs Conference. I support the idea of establishing a monitoring committee. It need not be an official body. It should be private, formed by veterans of the NAC who have faith in reform. We could join hands and try to make our voices heard. I must also say that Taiwan is trying to solve problems that have accumulated through four decades. You don't eradicate in three months all the problems experienced in forty years. We have to be patient and reasonable and try to exert positive and correct pressure so that people who are reform-minded in the KMT and the political opposition find us a helping force, not a hindrance.

There has been much debate over who are the real reformists. Many opposition friends came up and said, "We are the reformists, you are the conservatives. You resist change." I was unhappy about it. People like me are reformists too. We consider ourselves pragmatic reformists. We began to feel some of the people who were advocating reform were really romantic, or revolutionary. They are not down to earth. They ask too much, which you can not honestly achieve. After the conference I began to feel that the NAC was really a debate between idealistic reformists and realistic reformists. Of course, while stressing the significance of realism and pragmatism, I must also admit and accept that any reform would not have been possible without the existence and influence of some elements of idealism. Our reform should not be a struggle between the idealists and the realists. It should be a reform attempt of both. We must join hands to carry out reforms. There was a lot of talk after the NAC about who had won, the KMT or the DPP. In fact, the reformists won the conference, not either political party. Reform is not a zero-sum game. If we win, we all win.

Yao Chia-wen

The National Affairs Conference was a failure. It was doomed to failure because people in Taiwan don't agree on the meaning of the term "nation." What is the nation or state (*kuo-chia*) whose affairs the conference discussed? The participants in the conference disagreed on this question of definition at every session.

When we talked about the procedure to elect the president, the DPP insisted that the best way to elect a president is to allow the people to vote directly. Most of the KMT members, although not every one, say, "The twenty million people on Taiwan have no right to elect a president because this is the president of China, not the president of Taiwan." They insist that the more than one billion people in mainland China should have the power to vote for the president. Although at this time they cannot come to Taiwan to vote, the government can use one way or another, to delegate some people, such as members of the National Assembly, to vote on their behalf for the president of China.

The same issue affects the reform of parliament. Is our

parliament the parliament of Taiwan, or the parliament of China? The DPP insisted that every member of the new parliament after 1992 should be elected by the people on Taiwan. But most of the KMT members say, "Since this is not the parliament of Taiwan, we should allow some portion of the members to represent the mainland Chinese." Although we could accept the KMT position that all the old members should be retired by the end of 1991, we could not accept the KMT proposal to allow the KMT and the DPP to appoint a certain number of people to represent the whole country, the "at-large" delegates. When the KMT talked about the "country," they referred to China.

The issue also affects constitutional reform. The KMT insisted that we can only revise or amend the old Nanking Constitution. But the DPP insisted that we should not allow the Nanking Constitution to continue to be used in Taiwan since that is the constitution of China, not of Taiwan. We advocated a new constitution. But the KMT said there should not be a constitution just for Taiwan, because Taiwan is not a country.

We in the DPP think that our country is not the country of China. We also insist that Taiwan is not part of China, and was not even in 1947 when the current constitution was adopted (it took effect in 1948). In order to clarify whether Taiwan is part of China, on April 17, 1988, the DPP passed a resolution to state that Taiwan is not part of the PRC. We based our argument on the 1951 San Francisco peace treaty with Japan. At that time Japan gave up sovereignty over Taiwan, but did not say that sovereignty over Taiwan should be returned to China. When the Nanking Constitution was adopted in 1947, China did not have sovereignty over Taiwan, and it did not acquire sovereignty in 1951. So we can say that the Nanking Constitution has no right to be applied to the Taiwan area. Although in 1988 we used the phrase "Taiwan is not a part of the PRC" for special reasons, on the same basis we can also say that Taiwan is not a part of the ROC, especially if we refer to the Nanking Constitution of

1947. So the DPP insisted that we should adopt a new constitution only applicable to the area of Taiwan, and therefore only to the twenty million people of Taiwan.

After the NAC, people on Taiwan became increasingly concerned about the definition of the term nation or state. How big is our nation? How large is our population? Does our country have a territory of thirty-six thousand square kilometers or more than ten million square kilometers, which would include the territory of both the PRC and the Peoples' Republic of Mongolia? On October 7, 1990, the DPP National Conference in Taoyuan adopted a resolution stating that the "actual sovereignty" and "actual territory" of "our country" (we said "our country," not Taiwan) "does not extend to mainland China and outer Mongolia." It was a very sensitive issue at that time and the KMT even threatened to arrest me because I was the initial proposer of this resolution. Mr. Hong Yuh-Chin, who is here, called my wife and many others to say that if the DPP conference passes this resolution, Yao Chia-wen is to be arrested.

When my wife phoned to tell me of Mr. Hong's threat, I said this resolution must pass because it is so important. If the KMT threatens to arrest the person who initiated this resolution, that means the resolution is very important to the DPP. So the DPP decided to emphasize this issue. We think that this is the time to call on people to face the question of whether the sovereignty and territory of our country should include China and Mongolia.

If you go to any school in Taiwan, you'll see a very big map showing that the territory of the ROC includes Taiwan, the PRC, and the People's Republic of Mongolia—a total territory of ten million square kilometers. Many of our people who have visited the PRC noticed that their map is different. It does not include the Mongolian People's Republic. The PRC does not claim that Mongolia is a part of China. More and more people have tried to persuade the KMT to change our map to divide

Mongolia from the PRC. The KMT now advocates "one state, two governments," and charges that the DPP believes in "two states, two governments." The fact is, the DPP advocates "three states, three governments"—that is, three governments including the Mongolian People's Republic.

Since we believe that the sovereignty of this country does not include mainland China and Mongolia, it is clear that our legal system, our political system, our constitution, our parliament, and the procedure of presidential elections should be limited to this area. There should be no representatives of the mainland in our parliament. Twenty million people are enough to elect a president. As for our country's constitution, the only way acceptable to Taiwanese, acceptable to the DPP, and practical in light of the reality of Taiwan is to adopt a new constitution, not to use the Nanking Constitution any longer. Short of that kind of change, I don't think the KMT can carry out any change that can meet the needs of people.

Chang Chün-hung
The National Affairs Conference was a milestone in the postwar history of Taiwan. Its promise as a constitutional convention has not, to date, been fulfilled. And yet if seen in the longer sequence of political development on Taiwan, its significance remains.

The National Affairs Conference was called by President Lee Teng-hui to meet two urgent needs.

First, the society of Taiwan demands reform to create a structure that meets the current needs of the people and provides a viable long-term future. In the early decades after the Republic of China government moved its central organs and army to Taiwan in 1949, it could maintain its rule by blatant repression and by recourse to an anti-communist ideology. Early efforts at democratization, such as Lei Chen's *Free China* magazine, had an enlightened leadership, but the social conditions were not yet ripe for popular support. But mass organization was achieved with *Formosa* magazine (*Meilidao*) in 1979, and despite suppression and the imprisonment of its leadership, it was not defeated, but bloomed again in the mid-1980s. The people of Taiwan demand a representative and responsive government. This demand, fought for in the past with speeches and writings, election campaigns, street demonstrations, and imprisonment, has most recently been advanced by the opposition party with words and struggles in the impotent legislature—shouting matches, banners, overturned tables. This struggle culminated in the March 1990 student demonstrations, in effect a massive display of public indignation at the greed and arrogance of the "old thieves," the old National Assembly elected in China in 1947 that still tries to wield power over the fate of the people of Taiwan. To the adamant demands of the students Lee Teng-hui made the least possible response, promising a constitutional convention that would represent all sectors of the society.

Secondly, the ruling party, the Kuomintang, has found itself weighed down by the baggage of its past; the old structures of the government in China are an albatross around its neck. As time has passed, the National Assembly and legislature are more and more a source of ridicule, evidence of its lack of legitimacy and of a base in the people of Taiwan. Chiang Ching-kuo recognized this predicament; he shaped a new policy of Taiwanization in 1975, and quietly abandoned the call for retaking the mainland. As his successor in this endeavor, Lee Teng-hui has also inherited a mantle with some authority; but the old assemblies are for him even more of a burden, the "old garbage" that stinks. Therefore, it is obvious that the KMT is seeking a new formulation of its direction and its rule, and that it must revise its constitutional basis. It faces serious internal struggles, in which the reformers may be in the minority, because a majority of power holders may be desperately trying to cling to special privileges that belong to the old order.

Out of both these needs comes the process of constitutional reform. The KMT has realized that without such reform it could well face revolution. The demand of Taiwan's society is for peaceful evolution, if this is at all possible. The prosperity of Taiwan is the social basis for the demand for democracy; that prosperity must be maintained. Even while the KMT has degenerated from rule by the personal authority of dictators and security agencies into its present near-anarchy, the middle and professional classes have maintained stability.

The National Affairs Conference was a meeting outside of the established structure of the government. Our opposition movement for a long time has been hoping for such a new shaping of the government through such a meeting in order to avoid a revolution. I have been asked, "Why do you keep talking about constitutional legal reform rather than talking about social and environmental problems?" As political reformists, we are aware that the social problems and other problems in Taiwan are very severe. But we see that because of the obstacles in the issues of political representation and constitutionality, these problems cannot be solved.

In the National Affairs Conference we were a small minority. And because there was just such a small minority of us represented there, we had to ally with a broader range of forces. In the NAC, the DPP allied with three other forces. These were the so-called independents, that is non-members of the DPP and the KMT, the scholars from within Taiwan and overseas, and liberals within the KMT. Out of 150 members in the National Affairs Conference, the reform group numbered about 35. This group went through a long period of preparation. And this culminated in what we call the "Great Democratic Proposal" that we presented at the conference. In it, there were over ten concrete proposals, which we boiled down to basically four demands. First, rescind the Temporary Provisions and rewrite the constitution. Second, any new constitution or other major decision must be submitted to popular referendum. Third, the five-branch form of government must be revised and the government should be composed of one central representative body. Fourth, the president must be elected by direct popular election.

Before the beginning of the conference, the KMT had already agreed that the old legislators and national assemblymen would retire and that in the future the head of the province and the mayors would be elected. So therefore in the conference, facing the KMT strategy of diffusing the issues and scattering the issues, the reform group decided to focus its demands on direct election of the president by the people. The main reason why we focused on this issue is that we felt that with the death of Chiang Ching-kuo the authoritarian structure on a very basic level had been reduced to anarchy. There was no means for its renewal and continuation, and this could be a very dangerous situation. We felt that direct establishment of a presidency representing the people would be the best way to move through this transition.

This demand for direct election was agreed to by President Lee Teng-hui in a meeting with myself and party chairman Huang Hsin-chieh on April 2. It was again acquiesced by James Soong on the behalf of Lee Teng-hui during the NAC on July 2. The agreement was announced on July 3, the next-to-last day of the conference, by the chairman, Wu Feng-shan, and it was reiterated in a consensus statement of the presidium at the National Affairs Conference. The statement said, "The current method of electing the president should be changed. The president should be elected by citizens. The method and procedures for election should be enacted in accordance with legal procedures after consultation with all sectors of society."

After its announcement by Wu Feng-shan, the agreement was challenged by only a small number of people, some twenty or thirty, much less than one-third of those present. And it had been passed by the presidium. This agreement in this consensus cannot be overthrown by the KMT at a later point.

Professor Jason Hu says that this agreement at that time was not clear. I can say as a participant that it was entirely clear, entirely obvious to those present and there is no basis on which to overturn it. Not only those present in the hall, but the twenty million people of Taiwan who were watching these proceedings on nationally-broadcast television are witnesses to this fact. What's unfortunate is that the conservative forces within the KMT are now trying to turn back this promise bit by bit.

Actually, anti-reform forces tried to turn back the force of history even before the beginning of the conference, and tried to make a miscarriage of the conference. Just a few days before the start of the conference the anti-reform forces arrested Chen Chao-nan, a Taiwanese returning from the United States with an Austrian passport, on charges of sedition. It seemed that this was calculated to push the reform forces to withdraw from the conference. However, the reform forces chose a wiser road by putting out the news that if Chen were not released, they would boycott the dinner given by Hau Pei-tsun, who they thought was directly responsible for this.

Professor Hu also brought out another significant point. The anti-reform forces did not want to have any clear or binding result from this conference, so they opposed taking votes or making conclusions. But the reform forces insisted that there be at the very least a means for expressing conclusions. There were three days of procedural arguments over whether or not this conference was going to have conclusions, whether or not it was going to have voting, and the results of these discussions Professor Hu has himself quoted.

After these three days the reform group adopted a simple strategy. We demanded direct election of the president and put aside all other issues. On July 2, the KMT actually planned to deny all four requests of the reform group. The purpose of the conservative KMT forces was again to force the opposition, the reform group, to walk out of the convention, to make the convention a failure. We believe that they would have aimed next at Lee Teng-hui himself at the next election of KMT chairman.

In the end, consensus was achieved on the issue of direct election of the president. In the past the KMT refused to let the central organs of government undergo full re-election because they claimed that these represent national sovereignty over China. This excuse has already been rejected in the recent Judicial Yuan decision concerning the retirement of national assemblymen and Legislative Yuan members. But now it has appeared again as an excuse for opposing direct election of the president.

For the last forty years the myth of Chinese sovereignty has been the KMT's main excuse for refusing internal democracy. We don't see any sign that the KMT has any capacity to really exercise sovereignty over China. It seems that it continues to use this cry the same as a Taoist uses a paper talisman to ward off devils. What we are most concerned about now is that Taiwan, in effect, has no government. It has passed from an authoritarian period, but there is nothing to replace it. We must establish a presidency as a governmental core to resolve this problem.

Direct election of the president will certainly not cause any problem with mainland China. It will not cause any problem internally. It's the only way by which the current crises in Taiwan may be resolved peacefully.

When Yao Chia-wen was in prison with me, he often pointed out a very curious logic. If Taiwan is part of China, why is it that a president elected in Taiwan cannot be considered a president of China? If it's the case that a president elected in Taiwan cannot represent China, it only goes on to prove that Taiwanese are not Chinese. So, the major reason that we passed the resolution that Yao Chia-wen mentioned, that the actual sovereignty of the ROC does not extend to mainland China or

Mongolia, was that we wanted to resolve these central issues of democracy in Taiwan.

I'd like to quote the words of an elder in our struggle: "If democracy is in front, then Taiwan independence will fall behind. But, if the steps toward democracy are slowed, then Taiwan independence will surge ahead."

If we look at the present situation of reform within the KMT, we have to remember that in Chinese history, reform at court has never succeeded. The key obstacle has always been that the conservative forces, the forces against reform, were an entrenched special interest. For Lee Teng-hui to call upon forces within the KMT to seek reform means that reform certainly will fail. In order to achieve a successful reform under the conditions of Taiwan society, the president must seek the support of the people.

In Taiwan's four hundred years of history and in Chinese history, there has not been a case of the people's power coming to the fore, but now in Taiwan the people's power is strong and growing. There is no hope for reform unless this power of the people is used to move forward. And to use the people's power, the forces of the opposition party must be used as well. But since the NAC ended, the involvement of the opposition party in the process of reform has also been ended. If this force for peaceful reform is not reincorporated in the process, then what I fear, and what others fear, is that a process for revolution may come to the fore. The conservative forces say that if there is real democracy in Taiwan, China will attack Taiwan. But if Taiwan does not democratize, the major struggle will be from within. There will be a revolution for a new future. Taiwan's security cannot be confirmed by any amount of weapons. Its greatest security is in democracy. If it achieves internal democracy, then it will have security. And it will, in turn, have a great impact on China.

The Democratic Progressive Party is not so naive as to

believe that the reformers of the ruling party will continue to move forward on their own impetus. Instead of moving ahead with the multi-representational committee for rewriting the constitution that was recommended by the NAC, Lee Teng-hui has set up a committee under the Kuomintang alone, heavily loaded with the conservative forces. Every step forward will have to be coaxed and cajoled or coerced by the threat of mass protest. (Of course as soon as the step has been reached, the KMT claims the advance as its own enlightened intention.) The NAC merely established the outline of an agreement. The second step is the formulation of the new constitution. The third is the implementation of this new constitution through election of new legislators and government officials. Only when this third step has been reached can it be determined whether the National Affairs Conference succeeded or failed.

Looking to the future, many strange twists may lie ahead. The conservative forces within the KMT, as they lose ground to the mainstream "Taiwanized" KMT, may shout for "democracy" louder than anyone else, believing they can renew their power through alliance with Taiwanese front-men such as Lin Yang-kang. Lin Yang-kang has more of a popular base in his home area, Nantou; Lee Teng-hui is a technocrat with no experience in popular elections. But that will not delude experienced observers.

The benchmark of reform in the near future will be whether the president is elected directly by the people. The KMT wants to set up an electoral college "like the United States," but it is not to be believed that the KMT version will really represent a popular vote. Only with direct popular vote can vote-buying and other manipulation be prevented.

Ying-mao Kau
Three groups of people participated in the NAC: representatives of political parties, particularly the KMT and the DPP; the

so-called "representatives from various circles" including various occupational groups and so on; and the scholars, who were supposed to be objective and play a mediating or negotiating role in the process of discussion. I perceived myself in the last group. So here, I will present my personal and independent viewpoint.

My participation involved the conviction that Taiwan's political development is in a very serious bottleneck. Unless this bottleneck can be passed, the consequences could be very serious. As Ed Winckler suggested earlier, Taiwan is undergoing a transformation from an authoritarian or military dictatorship to a looser kind of political system. Such a process is difficult enough, but in the case of Taiwan, even though people don't want to talk about it, particularly the ruling party, there are two intervening variables that make the process even more complex. One is the ethnic conflict, involving the distribution of power between Taiwanese and mainlanders and the issues of independence and unification. The second is the new variable of the increasing interaction between Taiwan and the mainland. Beijing shows a mounting interest to interfere in domestic political developments in Taiwan. This is a very dangerous problem. So one can see why an extralegal, extraconstitutional conference was called to work out problems that cannot easily be worked out within the system.

Most conservatives argue in legal terms that there are constitutional restraints, so you cannot do something because the law does not allow it. In my judgment, this is missing the point because the fundamental issues are political ones.

At the NAC, a consensus was formed that the constitutional reform should be a major reform, not a minor reform. Because of the disagreement on whether to vote or not, it is difficult to establish how many people were in favor of what. But in my judgment most people were talking about major reform. I emphasize this point because I think that after the NAC, the

KMT now seems to be emphasizing minor reform.

Linked to constitutional reform, there was a consensus for abolishing the Temporary Provisions. Most of the KMT reformers and the DPP participants were in favor of this, and so were most of the scholars. But I continue to wonder whether the abolition of the Temporary Provisions will be unambiguously helpful. The original rationale for the Temporary Provisions was the internal Communist rebellion and the legitimate government's, the KMT's, attempt to suppress it. Once the Temporary Provisions are abolished, then what is the legal status of the relations between the legitimate ruling government on Taiwan and the legitimate ruling government on the mainland? Does it mean that the rebellion has succeeded so now let's forget about suppressing it? Does it mean that the CCP should be given an equal legal status so they can be active in Taiwan? Does it mean that now there are two governments and that both are legitimate in China? So my question is whether the elimination of the Temporary Provisions really opens a beautiful door for constitutional reform, or opens the lid on another can of worms involving the unification and independence issue.

On the issue of electing a president directly or indirectly, or adopting as a compromise an American electoral-college type system, I think the key point is how the choice of system will affect the future. To what extent will a newly popularly elected president have more power to break the bottleneck I talked about earlier? For most of the reformists the conviction is quite strong that this is the way to do it. But the more conservative side, particularly within the KMT, is very reluctant. This could prolong the political stalemate we discussed this morning, and as a result create a greater political crisis.

The issue of whether to have quotas for mainland and overseas Chinese representation involves both legal and philosophical questions. Many Taiwanese are asking, if you are going to invite thirty million overseas Chinese to be represented in Taiwan, over and above twenty million Taiwanese, then who are the majority and who are the minority? If you are going to have a large number of people representing the mainland, are they not going to overpower the locally elected delegates? These are real concerns, and unless the KMT thinks seriously about this, they may have trouble preserving the principle of representation for the mainland and for overseas Chinese. Recently, there has been talk of having as many as two-fifths of the representatives in the category of National Constituency at Large, as Professor Hu mentioned earlier. If you set that quota so high, is it going to overshadow the local electorate and create political problems?

A resolution was adopted, without dissent I believe, at the third session of the NAC, calling for a non-partisan, broadly based constitutional reform monitoring committee. My impression is that this was introduced by the chairman of the session and adopted with no dissent whatever. However, it was totally ignored after the conference. I find this unfortunate. I want to emphasize my dismay because scholars in particular maintain very high expectations and hopes that the extraconstitutional NAC can perform an important political role in breaking the bottleneck in the way of democratization. If the government, or the political leadership, refuses to take this seriously and tries to water down the NAC's conclusions, I think the backlash is going to be severe. The credibility of the government, of the KMT, and particularly of the president may fall into question.

Recently a National Unification Commission was established under the president's office with great fanfare. I believe this commission is very much contrary to the spirit and the intent of the NAC. As you know there were five major topics identified for the NAC: (1) reform of parliament, (2) reorganization of the central government, (3) institutionalization of local government, (4) constitutional reform, and (5) relations between the two sides of the Taiwan Straits. Constitutional reform was the major topic, taking up most of the effort at the NAC and logically deserving highest priority. But after the NAC, priorities seemed to be shifted and the National Unification Commission was established quickly. My feeling is that a more even-handed policy is called for by establishing two commissions, one dealing with constitutional reform, the other dealing with the relationship between the two sides of the Taiwan Straits. If this approach were taken, the NAC results would have greater credibility. This still could be done. Some scholars are talking about it quite seriously.

In conclusion let me raise a point that I raised at the congressional hearing last week. I am concerned at the mounting interest of the PRC in playing a role in internal political developments on Taiwan. As I said, internal political reform is difficult enough, and now there is this new element coming in. Of course there is also increasing interaction between Taiwan and mainland China. A lot of people visit there, and recently the KMT decided that high officials within the KMT will also be permitted to visit mainland China, including even members of the Central Committee. When those people visit Beijing, are they visiting their relatives, or are they meeting behind closed doors with high officials in Beijing, and what are they talking about?

Recently Red Cross officials from mainland China went to Chinmen for negotiations on the repatriation of illegal immigrants. This an important technical issue, but I think it has raised a lot of questions in the minds of Taiwanese. What are these people doing? Are they making any secret deals? This is an alarming issue because unless internal political stability can be maintained, the ruling party is going to face serious problems.

There are people in Taiwan who would like to play the so-called PRC card, the Beijing card, in order to balance against sentiment for Taiwan independence. I can understand this kind of urge, but in my view it is a very dangerous game. It has the possibility of stimulating internal political unrest and leading to large-scale political violence in Taiwan. If that should happen, Beijing may intervene in fact and the very people who are playing the China card may be victimized in the process. I sincerely hope the people on Taiwan will have the wisdom to face up to this kind of difficult problem and come up with a better, more constructive solution.

—Floor Discussion—

Hung-mao Tien

Earlier, Yao Chia-wen and Chang Chün-hung emphasized the importance of popular election of the president. And Professor Jason Hu said that in the National Affairs Conference there was no clear consensus on the method of electing of the president. I feel compelled to make some comment on that, because not only did I participate in the National Affairs Conference, but I was the one who introduced the procedural motion from the floor in favor of popular election of the president. And I also served on the NAC Presidium of fifteen members, where the same issue was raised and where there was considerable discussion.

The presidium established the ground rule that the chairperson who presided over a general session of the National Affairs Conference could exercise the prerogative of indicating whether or not there appeared to be a consensus on a given issue. Wu Feng-shan, who chaired the session on institutional reform of national government, summarized what appeared to him to be the consensus on popular election of the president and announced it. At that point Lin Tung, who happened to be sitting next to me, raised a strong objection. But except for him, there were few, if any, other objections.

Immediately after that session, the presidium met to discuss the controversy regarding Mr. Wu's announcement as well as the issue of popular election of the president. None of the fifteen presidium members questioned that there was a consensus on popular election of the president. The consensus was precisely what Chang Chün-hung said earlier, that the president must be elected by the citizens with the details to be subject to consultation by all parties concerned. As a person who was involved in the deliberation process, I believe the consensus on popular election of the president was clear, and there was no ambiguity about it.

Jason C. Hu
I think I have to clarify something. When I said there was no clear consensus, if I remember correctly, I said there was no consensus on the *direct* election of the president. Now, there *was* no clear consensus on the *direct* election of the president. Wu Feng-shan's exact words were, "The current method of electing the president should be changed. The president should be elected by citizens. The method and procedures for election should be enacted in accordance with legal procedures after consultation with all sectors of society."

This was the original translation. But when you say "with all sectors of society," people may have misunderstood it as referring to political parties. What was really meant was consultations with all concerned sections of our society. This was the conclusion suggested by the chairman on that day. It contained no reference to the direct election. The formulation permits an electoral college because it would still be elected by all citizens.

The controversy of the day was not just about the substance of the statement, but also about the procedure. There was a question of whether the chairman, even if supported by the presidium, has the right to summarize a discussion at 12:15 p.m., just as everyone was getting ready to go to lunch. Just at that point he stood up, made his statement, and said, "That's it, meeting adjourned." People were not ready for such conclusions, and I think it was not truly democratic in practice.

Michael Wei (Associate Professor, Graduate Institute of Social Welfare, National Chung-Cheng University)
Mr. Chang Chün-hung quoted a very interesting saying: "If democracy marches forward, Taiwan independence will fall behind. But if democracy is behind, Taiwan independence will march forward." My question is, do you think the following things can be seen as examples of democracy: lifting the ban on political party organization; lifting the ban on establishing new newspapers; and announcing that by the end of 1991, the old legislators will be out of the arena? Do you think these things can be regarded as democracy? If not, what is your definition of democracy? Do you imply the direct election of president is the real meaning of democracy?

Chang Chün-hung
The examples given can be said to be democratic. Certainly the agreement for a new constitution and new election of the legislature and the National Assembly are a promise of democracy. And it only took forty-three years to get there! But in the current circumstance in which an authoritarian ruler has passed away, we're now really in a situation of anarchy in dealing with social and economic issues. And as I see it, the only way to resolve this securely and quickly is through direct election of the president.

Chi Su
I think it's safe to say that no one in this room is against democracy. Actually, I found Mr. Chang Chün-hung's speech quite appealing this morning. However, I think independence is an entirely different matter. I would like to hear Mr. Yao's assessment of the PRC's policy toward Taiwan, as well as U.S. policy toward the Taiwan question.

Parris Chang

Our discussion has so far failed to mention one very fundamental issue which, I think, affects all the other issues we are talking about. What I have in mind is the issue of ethnicity in Taiwan's politics, the conflict between Taiwanese and mainlanders. Discussion of this used to be taboo, but from the beginning of this year it has become very prominent. And only when we address this issue will many of our other questions make sense.

Earlier Ed Winckler declared that the issue of parliamentary democracy versus presidential democracy is meaningless. It's meaningful only when you address the question of ethnicity because the Taiwanese certainly think that the president ought to be elected directly by the people. Lots of mainlanders want parliamentary democracy because they don't want the Taiwanese to seize power with a presidency elected directly by the people.

I also disagree with Ed's view that the last forty years of Taiwan politics are correctly characterized as a "military dictatorship." I would say the term "colonial regime" more accurately describes Taiwan's politics. But it is in the process of changing, of course. We have to address this issue. A group of outsiders came from mainland China and lorded over the local people, and they still refuse to give up or share power with the majority. So many of the issues we talk about center around this.

Hong Yuh-Chin

Yao Chia-wen earlier made a remark concerning my phone call to Mrs. Yao. The subject matter concerned the passage of a resolution by the DPP stating that the sovereignty of the Republic of China does not extend to the mainland and Mongolia. What I did was make a phone call to Mrs. Yao to say that Premier Hau Pei-tsun had already made it clear in the Legislative Yuan that the passage of a resolution like that might infringe the law and entail the risk of arrest. I merely tried to communicate that to her. Maybe there was some miscommunication between either myself and Mrs. Yao, or between Mrs. Yao and Mr. Yao. The Republic of China now is trying to follow the rule of law, and not arrest anyone except according to law. Maybe there is some fear lingering in the minds of Mrs. Yao and Mr. Yao, and if that is so, I hope that it will be removed. For the sake of democracy, I hope the political opposition will get stronger. Some question was expressed earlier regarding lack of implementation of the reform recommendations of the National Affairs Conference. The KMT's Constitutional Reform Policy Planning Group has prepared a draft timetable for its own work, which I will make available to the participants in the conference.

Attachment provided by Hong Yuh-Chin
Constitutional Reform Policy Planning Group
Work Plan:
July 1990–May 1991
I. Legal System Sub-Group: August 1990–January 1991
   1. Issues concerning National Assembly: August–September 1990
   2. Issues concerning Control Yuan: August–October 1990
   3. Issues concerning the timing and size of the second session Central Representative Bodies: August–October 1990
   4. Issues concerning overseas Chinese, professional groups, and women's delegates: August–November 1990
   5. Issues concerning the National at Large Delegate system: August–November 1990
   6. Issues concerning popular election of the president and vice-president: August–December 1990
   7. Issues concerning the relationship between the president, the Executive Yuan, and the Legislative Yuan: August–November 1990

8. Issues regarding the method for revising the ROC Constitution (including the Temporary Provisions): August–September 1990
9. Issues concerning the declaration of the end of the Period of Mobilization to Suppress Rebellion: August–January 1991
10. Issues concerning abolition of the Temporary Provisions for the Period of Mobilization to Suppress Rebellion: August 1990–April 1991

II. Working Sub-Group: August 1990–April 1991
   1. Reference Materials Unit: August–October 1990
   2. Public Outreach Unit: August 1990–April 1991
   3. Coordination Unit: August 1990–April 1991
   4. Bureaucratic Reorganization Unit: August 1990–January 1991
   5. Local Government Unit: August 1990–January 1991

U.S. Policy in a Time of Rapid Political Change on Taiwan

David Dean

Rapid political change on Taiwan began very recently. Prior to 1986, Taiwan's political situation was rather stagnant. But in the fall of 1986, when the late president Chiang Ching-kuo gave his interview to Katherine Graham, the publisher of the *Washington Post*, he described five significant political reforms that he intended to implement. They included reform of the Legislative Yuan, but even more importantly the legalization of opposition political parties. At one point after that date, the late president told me that he had hoped to institute some of those reforms even earlier, much earlier in fact, but various developments, both external and internal, had prevented him from doing this. In any event, he did announce those reforms, and since his death they have been implemented gradually by President Lee Teng-hui.

These reforms have come about in a very short period of time. They have affected everyone who lives in Taiwan. The effects are certainly seen very clearly in the press, which publishes virtually anything now. They are seen clearly in the attitudes of the political parties. To some it's disconcerting; they feel cast adrift. Change has been so rapid that they don't know what to do. Others feel that the change is not fast enough. In any case, there's no way of stopping the change. It is like a huge river running through rapids. The only thing that can be done is to steer around the rapids and try to direct the society in a way that's going in the right direction.

This change from an authoritarian system to a newly evolving system has been coupled with a sharp increase in wealth, with huge problems in the environment and with traffic gridlock, and with other changes in the society and the economy, and so it has been a very unsettling period.

In this setting, what was and is U.S. policy? First, I think I have to provide a little background. Ever since 1971, when Henry Kissinger made his secret visit to Beijing, it has been known in Taipei that the U.S. was moving toward recognition of the PRC. It was clear that this was happening when the U.S. established a liaison office in Beijing and when various high-level visits took place. It wasn't a coincidence, I believe, that Henry Kissinger was in Beijing at the very time that the United Nations was voting to replace the Republic of China with the PRC as the occupant of the China seat. So the sword of Damocles, you might say, was hanging over the Republic of China on Taiwan.

Speaking of the UN, I was in our political section in our embassy in Taipei in 1967. We tried at that time to persuade the Chinese government to accept the concept of dual recognition in the United Nations. I went around to everybody, pestering them, talking to them about this, trying to influence the top government leaders and politicians. Usually I got the response, "Better a piece of broken jade than a whole tile." It was rejected as a matter of principle. That was the mind-set of the times. Now I suspect people wish that the response in 1967 had been different. Perhaps if there had been some form of dual recognition accepted by the membership of the United Nations, Taipei might still have its representation there, at least in the General Assembly. But that's history.

Getting back to the development of the U.S. relationship with the mainland, I recall the incident when Secretary Vance visited Beijing in August 1977. He tried to get Deng Xiaoping to accept a liaison office, a consulate general, or some form of U.S. official presence in Taipei at the same time that the U.S. went ahead with its recognition of the PRC. Deng characterized Vance's visit as a step backward in the relationship between the U.S. and the PRC. He implied that the two previous administrations, Ford and Nixon, had agreed to proceed with recognition without these conditions. Subsequently Zbigniew Brzezinski, President Carter's National Security Adviser, visited Beijing in May 1978 and initiated negotiations with the PRC for U.S. recognition.

Those negotiations started in the summer of 1978, and they were secret. The State Department was basically unaware of what was going on, or the terms. Certainly Congress and the public did not know. When the announcement on diplomatic relations was made on December 15, 1978, there was consternation in many circles. That was true in Taiwan because even though they had feared this development for a long time, it happened very suddenly. And there was consternation in Congress. They had not been consulted, and they did not know what the terms were or what the implications would be for an ongoing relationship with Taiwan.

There was some concern within the administration as well. It felt very nervous about the new policy. The Carter Administration was trying hard to move ahead and cement the relationship with the PRC, so it was deeply concerned about anything that Taipei did that might affect the new relationship with the mainland. You could say that from that point on, U.S. policy toward Taiwan was reactive. Reactive in the sense that it was so deeply concerned about the relationship with Beijing that Taiwan was considered mainly as a factor in that relationship. There wasn't a positive policy toward Taiwan itself.

As you know, Congress took a strong hand in crafting the Taiwan Relations Act. When we established the American Institute in Taiwan and Taiwan set up the Coordination Council for North American Affairs, it was a very tentative and very difficult type of relationship. The Foreign Ministry in Taipei was trying to regain a measure of officiality in the relationship. Business circles both in Taiwan and in the U.S. were worried about their assets. Everybody was worried about the future.

What would happen to the relationship? Would it go downhill and virtually disappear? Or could it be preserved?

Things got progressively worse, continuing during the subsequent presidential election campaign. Ronald Reagan, the Republican candidate, gave a press conference in August 1980 and mentioned the desirability of having some form of official relationship with Taiwan at least ten or twelve times. He used the word "officiality" throughout his talk. The Republican vice-presidential candidate, George Bush, was visiting Beijing and received a very cold reception because of that press conference. That caused the regime in Beijing to be very tough on the United States in terms of our relationship with Taiwan. This attitude of toughness manifested itself in a Beijing demand for a moratorium on arms sales from the U.S. to Taiwan, and eventually led to President Reagan's decision not to sell the F/X advanced fighter plane to Taiwan.

The situation led in turn to the August 17, 1982, Communiqué, in which the U.S. agreed to lower gradually the amount of arms sales to Taiwan and not to exceed the quantity and quality of previous arms sales.

That, you might say, was a low point in the U.S. relationship with Taiwan, and I think it was also a turning point. From that point on things began to improve. There was a great deal of effort on the part of many of us to try to restore some element of trust and confidence between both sides. At first it was very tentative. But I'm happy to say that over the course of the last eight years that initial beginning has resulted in a major improvement in the atmosphere of our bilateral relations. Although U.S. policies are still reactive to PRC pressures, they are less so than before.

There has been a growing focus in the U.S. on human rights policy. This was evidenced primarily by Congressman Solarz's interest in this subject, and by Congressman Leach, Senator Kennedy, and others who wanted to see more of a human rights policy accepted in Taiwan. I equate the human rights drive with the drive toward more democracy. Basically that's what these members of Congress were looking for, for more democratic reforms in Taiwan. And Solarz certainly was quite effective holding various congressional hearings, trying through letters and other communications to convince the government in Taipei that a more democratic policy and a more liberal policy was in everyone's interest.

Although criticized by some who said he was interfering in Taiwan's internal affairs, and by others said he should pay more attention to what was happening in the United States, I think Mr. Solarz definitely made a difference. And I think that the difference was a big plus.

Another aspect of U.S. relations with Taiwan has been trade policy. The U.S. trade deficit with Taiwan during this period grew and grew, until in 1987 it reached nineteen billion dollars. This was an enormous figure, second only to our deficit with Japan, and at a time when a great deal of congressional attention was being focused on the U.S. trade deficit. There was enormous pressure on the government in Taiwan to take measures to lower the deficit. To their credit, they did. They virtually took more measures than any other government. Certainly many more measures than Japan ever took. President Lee came out with a trade action plan, which was a very useful vehicle to chart out the steps that would be taken to lower the trade imbalance.

Among other things, it called for market diversification. Earlier, 50 percent of Taiwan's exports had been sent to the United States. By last year, the figure had gone below 35 percent and was still dropping. Taiwan has developed alternate markets in Southeast Asia, Eastern Europe, and many other parts of the world, even on the mainland. So their trade is shifting and is not focused solely on one market or captive to the economic health of that one economy. There were disputes, as you are aware—such as the Great Turkey War and pressures for currency appreciation. But generally speaking both sides benefitted.

In addition the financial and economic ministries in Taiwan gradually restructured part of their own domestic economy, placing more emphasis on domestic consumption instead of overemphasizing foreign trade.

U.S. policy in other areas was still very tentative toward Taiwan, still reactive and still focused on the mainland and not on Taiwan. Then came the Tiananmen massacre. This as you know caused a genuine feeling of outrage, disappointment, and horror in the United States. Congressional reaction was strong. President Bush tried to limit the damage to the bilateral relationship between Washington and Beijing. He felt it was important to have positive, relatively friendly relations with the mainland rather than to have a negative, hostile relationship. He feared that if the sanctions proposed by Congress and by other nations succeeded, the mainland might drift into a more hostile posture, which would have consequences for other places in East Asia, including the Taiwan Straits, the Korean peninsula, and Indochina and Southeast Asia.

At the same time, Taiwan's influence in the world was growing. Even though not complete and even though proceeding perhaps slowly in some respects, the political reforms have captured the imagination not only of Americans, but of Europeans and Southeast Asians as well. So Taiwan's image, which is already quite strong because of its trade surpluses and its economic power, was improved also by political change. Taiwan gained more respect from other societies because of these political reforms, and because the political reforms seem to be proceeding in a relatively peaceful way.

At the same time Taiwan was adopting a flexible foreign policy. Instead of the negative "Three-No" policy (no official contacts, no negotiations, no concessions), it was beginning to have a great deal of interchange with the mainland. First, hundreds of thousands of people went to the mainland on family visits or tours. Then came trade. Trade soared in the 1987–88 period; it fell somewhat in 1989, but it's climbing again. And also investments. Not large scale if one leaves out Wang Yung-ching's possible Formosa Plastics plant, but small-scale investments of perhaps one million dollars, where an entrepreneur would pick up his entire shoe plant, with the machinery and everything else, and send it over to Xiamen in Fujian with his managers and set up a factory there, because labor rates were $60 a month instead of $600 a month on Taiwan. Just before Tiananmen, Shirley Kuo, who was then the Minister of Finance, traveled to Beijing to attend the Asian Development Bank annual meeting. She was the first ROC minister to travel to Beijing since 1949.

Taiwan's prestige is increasing with a more flexible foreign policy, new contacts with the mainland, economic strength, huge foreign exchange reserves, and political reforms. But the U.S., although impressed, has still been rather tentative about its policy toward Taiwan. Taiwan, for example, wants to join the General Agreement on Tariffs and Trade (GATT). Members of Congress have written letters to the president endorsing Taiwan's entry into GATT. But the White House is still tentative because of their concern over Beijing's reaction. Beijing has made it known that they want to get into GATT first before there's any consideration of Taiwan's entry.

Similarly, there have been discussions about Taiwan's joining the Asia Pacific Economic Council, which is Australian Premier Hawke's initiative to create an Asia-Pacific economic group. Eventually I think Taiwan will get into GATT and into the Asia Pacific Economic Council as well. I think that over time the reactive nature of U.S. policy will gradually weaken, and it will be less influenced by developments in the PRC.

It's hard to say what U.S. policy toward Taiwan is going to be five years from now. A great deal depends on the progress

Taiwan makes politically and economically. And a great deal depends on what its relationship is with the mainland. And indeed, what U.S. relationships with the mainland are. If you endorse the premise that the mainland's leadership, whoever they may be, will be preoccupied for the foreseeable future with their own domestic economic and political problems, then it's possible that their influence abroad will be considerably less than it has been.

This is particularly true at a time when the East/West confrontation seems to be disappearing, and at a time when Beijing cannot use its relationship with Moscow to try to force concessions from Washington. So while I have difficulty in foreseeing exactly what U.S. policy is likely to be toward Taiwan in the future, I think it will be better, at least to a modest degree, than it has been in the past. In the past we have wanted Taipei to contribute, for instance, to the Brady Plan for debt relief for certain Latin American nations. Or we've wanted them to help with funds in one place or another. And they themselves offered to help finance the deployment of troops to Saudi Arabia. But the U.S. and others have been unwilling to acknowledge this type of help and give Taipei a participating role. I think that's likely to change, not right away, but as time goes by.

Certainly in the last few years Taiwan's relationships with other countries—European countries, Southeast Asian countries, Japan, and the United States—have gotten much thicker, much broader, much more meaningful to all the participants. It is a process, I believe, that is likely to continue. And it will in the long run influence U.S. policy.

—Floor Discussion—

The Chairman (Harvey J. Feldman)
As you were speaking, I was reminded of a rarely noticed aspect of the triangular relationship between Washington, Beijing, and

Taipei. It's no secret that at several points over the last decade the PRC has approached the United States asking that it take a more active role in pushing Taiwan into a negotiation on reunification. The U.S., wisely I believe, has always begged off doing that, saying in effect, "No, no. That's not our role." But when you were talking about trade and footwear factories moving to the mainland, I thought that after all, the United States really is pushing the two sides together. Why are these footwear factories moving to the mainland? Surely it is in order to better penetrate the U.S. market.

Lynn Miles (Founder, International Committee for Human Rights in Taiwan)
Would you be able to shed any light on the timing of the December 1978 announcement establishing relations, given the impact it had on domestic events in Taiwan? I think you foresaw it coming, and probably advised Washington one way or the other.

The Chairman
May I answer that? I was Director of the Office of Republic of China Affairs in the State Department at the time. And believe me, there was nobody who was making policy on this issue in the White House who even knew that an election was coming up in Taiwan. I know it became a myth among the political opposition at the time, and perhaps some members of the DPP believe it, that this was done intentionally, that Jimmy Carter picked December 15, 1978, to make this announcement in order to forestall an election in which the opposition groups were bound to score heavily. Believe me, Jimmy Carter knew nothing about elections in Taiwan.

I'll tell you a funny story. We kept on saying that you had to give Chiang Ching-kuo time to prepare the people. You couldn't just spring it on him. And so I was asked once, "What is the minimum amount of time that we have to give Chiang? How much advance notice does he need in order to prepare the people for the announcement on normalization?'' And I said, ''Well, it should be a month, but the absolute minimum would be not less than two weeks.''

December 15, 1978, was a Friday and I came to the office as usual at 8:30. At a quarter of nine I'm called up to Assistant Secretary Dick Holbrooke's office and I'm told that at 9:00 that night, 9:00 Friday evening Washington time, Jimmy Carter is going on television to announce normalization. I burst out laughing. I said, ''Dick, this is crazy. You're pulling my leg. Come on, what's really happening?'' He said, ''No, no. He's going to announce on December 15, that on January 1 we're going to establish formal relations with the PRC. So that way he gets the two weeks notice that you always said Chiang Ching-kuo needs.''

Parris Chang
In recent months it has been stated that if the DPP moves in certain directions, or if the ROC government does certain things, the PRC might use force against Taiwan. We know that the Taiwan Relations Act has certain provisions on this particular matter. If the PRC were to do something like Iraq did against Kuwait, what would the American position be?

David Dean
Let me answer with typical indirection. I cannot visualize the United States under present circumstances, or European countries, or Japan, or other countries that have diplomatic relations with Beijing, I cannot visualize them breaking those relations in order to establish relations with an independent Taiwan. Therefore, if Taiwan were to try to go it on its own, without any international support, it would leave the PRC with a pretty clear field to do several things. They don't have to

grab it like Iraq grabbed Kuwait. All they would have to do would be to use propaganda warfare to raise the tension levels in the Taiwan Straits; perhaps threaten a blockade, send shipping insurance rates sky high, and make foreign carriers very reluctant to go in that area. They could do a lot of things short of an outbreak of fighting. And all of these things would be disadvantageous, I think, not only to Taiwan, but to its relationships with other countries. Other countries would think that Taiwan had brought this down on its own head, creating problems for Japan, problems for the United States. I personally think that Japan, and maybe the U.S. too, likes the status quo, and is not in favor of seeing either side endanger that status quo.

As for the Taiwan Relations Act and whether or not Congress would act to carry out its provisions, I think that depends on the circumstances. It depends on our force deployments, for example in Saudi Arabia against the Iraqi problem. It depends on public attitudes in the United States. It depends on presidential leadership. It depends on the U.S. economic position; if we're in a deep recession it could be a factor. It depends on the attitudes of the Soviet Union and other nations. So it's a very complicated issue. I don't think you can discuss the issue of Taiwan independence without looking at what's happening in every other part of the world, because it affects so many other countries too.

The Chairman
The basic substratum of U.S. policy from the time of the Shanghai Communiqué on is that the question of Taiwan is to be solved by the Chinese on both sides of the Taiwan Straits. And this we have understood to mean that neither side can force a solution on the other; that if there is to be a solution, it must be one that is agreed to by both parties. Which means no invasion, and no unilateral declaration of independence.

Parris Chang
Some have said that independence is something you can do but
cannot talk about. Now the Taipei government is moving step by
step in that direction. If the PRC, down the road ten years, says
we have waited long enough, we want to talk about
reunification—what would be the United States' position?

David Dean
There are two points here. The first is the definition of the word
"independence." I was talking with some of our colleagues
earlier today. Taiwan is not ruled by Beijing. It is not ruled by
the United States, Japan, or any other nation. It rules itself.
Some of you may think the government is doing a great job.
Others may hope that it would change more rapidly. But
basically it rules itself. It is, by that definition, independent. I
suppose that what you are talking about is not the de facto
situation that now exists, but a gradual trend over the years
toward a de jure declaration of independence, or even gradual
moves toward establishing a separate sovereign entity
without consulting the PRC. Then, will the PRC see this drift,
and will they become nervous and undertake action? I don't
know.

When I got back from Taiwan last December, the Chinese
ambassador in Washington asked me to come by for a private
lunch. He asked about the independence movement in Taiwan.
He was concerned with two things. First, he was concerned with
the policy of Taiwanization, which President Lee has continued
as you can see from the composition of his cabinet and other
appointments. I think that they were concerned that would lead
to separatism, or to a trend of drifting apart. He also was
worried about the leaders of the independence movement and
what their position would be—whether they would gain political
strength as time went by to a point where they would also wish
to declare a separate nation.

Although Beijing now insists on "one country, two systems," that doesn't mean that that's what they're going to get. That doesn't mean that that's the ultimate solution. It doesn't even mean there's going to be a solution. If there is a solution, it may be something entirely different because it has to be a solution that people who live on Taiwan can live with and are comfortable with.

I don't know what the outcome is going to be. I think they will have to consider very carefully, if they ever think of using force, what the other implications may be for them, both externally and internally.

Maysing Yang (Director, Asian-Pacific Council on Democracy) Didn't Congressional Resolution 293, pushed by Congressman Solarz, say in the last paragraph that it is the sense of Congress that, in determining the future of Taiwan, the wishes of people on the island should be taken into account to effect a democratic mechanism? If that is so, why should the future of Taiwan be decided by the people of the mainland? In the case of Puerto Rico, it is the people in Puerto Rico who vote in referendums, not the people of the U.S.

The Chairman
Let me make a clarification. When I said that the basic substratum of U.S. policy was that the issue has to be decided by the freely given acceptance of the people on both sides of the Taiwan Straits, I was describing what U.S. policy was and is. I didn't say it was my policy, or David's policy. It's U.S. policy. And the resolution that you have read I don't think contradicts that. What it basically says is that any solution that is proposed has to be agreed to by the people who live on Taiwan, recapitulating language of the Taiwan Relations Act. But there is no point in forgetting what U.S. policy was and is.

Paul S.P. Hsu
My question is addressed to both of you. In your opinion, what is the PRC's view of the fact that Taiwan is not subject to their jurisdiction now, and toward the theory that Taiwan may not be subject to their sovereignty?

The Chairman
I know of no one better qualified to answer that question than Paul Hsu. What's your view?

Paul S.P. Hsu
Well, I think it's a fact that Taiwan is not subject to their jurisdiction. The question is, how do they accept that fact? Do they accept it very well, or do they accept it with resentment? Or do they accept it with reluctance, or do they accept it with pleasure?

David Dean
I think they accept it because their proposal, which you may not like and which may not suit your conditions, but their proposal for Taiwan is similar to that for Hong Kong. In other words a separate society, a separate system. I think they have a divided mind on this. They are realistic enough to know that you have a free market society that works. That your own progress economically and now politically is much more apparent than their own. So there are probably some overtones of envy mixed into their feelings.

Deng initially hoped that the standard of living on the mainland would rise to a point that it was not too far away from that of the people on Taiwan, but that's not happening. What's happening is that the standard of living is soaring on Taiwan and it's increasing very little, if at all, on the mainland. So he's not going to be able to entice Taiwan into some sort of relationship based on everybody's standard of living being equal. He's a realist. At the same time they can be emotionally involved with the territorial imperative and feel that Taiwan is part of their territory. They realize that there is nothing much they can do about it, but they are still going to try, in terms of trying to get Indonesia to recognize them, to get Singapore to recognize them, to get Saudi Arabia to recognize them, perhaps Korea. They'll do their best to try to isolate Taiwan diplomatically. Well, that isolation isn't working very well because of Taiwan's economic strength and other strengths.

Paul S.P. Hsu
Do you see a sense of urgency on their part?

David Dean
I don't think so, except for the fear that Taiwanization and the independence movement may cause trouble in the future. You would think, logically and rationally, that would make them come to some compromise to change their position on "one government, two systems," to come out for perhaps "one China, two regions," which has been suggested by Premier Hau Pei-tsun. I don't know if it will cause them to do that. It may, over time. They may find that it is more in their advantage, as time goes by, to draw upon Taiwan's technical expertise, managerial pool, capital resources, trade, and know-how.

A lot depends on what happens in the mainland itself, within its leadership, where I'm sure that Taiwan is a subject of fierce arguments when it comes up. But I don't think that they spend every waking minute wondering what they should do about Taiwan. They have so many other problems that preoccupy them that they don't have that luxury.

Taiwan Year 2000

Chu Yun-han

My assignment is to outline the course of political development
in Taiwan in the coming decade, and from there to project what
the future Taiwanese politics will look like around the year 2000.
Projection and forecasting is not an area we are good at. Social
scientists tend to cling to their accumulated knowledge, which
might be easily overtaken by the pace and complexity of
present-day change. On the other hand, I don't think the
politicians are good prognosticators either. Politicians tend to
inject their own desirable outcomes and partisan preferences into
their projection. But they sometimes do have a kind of
innovative vision that helps stretch our imagination beyond the
realm of extrapolation.

When we ask what the Taiwan polity will look like in the
year 2000, essentially we are asking a three-part question. First,
what kind of international status will be accorded to Taiwan?
Will Taiwan be recognized as not only a de facto independent
state but also a de jure one? Or will the present status quo
continue, no matter how confusing and ambiguous?

The second question is, what kind of political regime will
emerge in the coming decade? Will the old regime be thoroughly
transformed and will the new democracy be consolidated? Or
will the drive for political reform gradually run out of steam so
that substantial residual authoritarian elements will remain? Will
the populace and the opposition settle for half-measure reforms?
Also, can we, based on the experiences of some Latin American
countries and the Soviet Union, entirely rule out the possibility
for regression, for the reimposition of a new authoritarian rule?

Third, what kind of party system, party leadership, and
electoral politics will have emerged by the year 2000? Will the
KMT still be in power? Will KMT split into two camps? Is
Taiwan going to have a third significant party? What is the

implication of generational turnover as people now in their forties and fifties take charge? What kind of social cleavages will be translated into partisan competition?

Recognizing the importance of the other two, I will focus primarily on the second question, for the most fundamental question remains the emergence and consolidation of new democracy.

Two kinds of factors are involved. The first are structural factors, which are important in their own right, but don't necessarily dictate the outcome. There are three kinds of structural constraints that are clearly relevant. The first is the evolution of the global and regional political-economic systems, including the future foreign policies pursued by the United States, Japan, and other important regional players toward Taiwan and PRC. If Taiwan can continue to find itself in a congenial international environment for its export-oriented industrialization, the democratic transition will have a better chance to run its full course. On the other hand, if the liberal international trade regime gradually gives way to protectionism and the hardening of fortressed trading blocs, Taiwan will be forced to reorient its development strategy as well as external economic relationship. This would create stronger economic incentives for deepening its economic dependence on mainland China possibly at the cost of Taiwan's political autonomy. In that case, polarized conflict over the issue of independence versus reunification would intensify and become entangled with issues of economic growth and distribution.

The second important external factor will be mainland China's policies and strategies toward Taiwan. This depends as much on the future political-economic development in mainland China as any initiatives taken by Taiwan. Will Beijing continue to tolerate Taiwan's current trend toward Taiwanization and democratization given the possibility that the political transition might activate the independence movement? Will coastal provinces, which benefit most from the accelerated economic exchanges across the straits and have a greater stake in maintaining a peaceful and constructive relation with Taiwan, acquire a more tolerant attitude toward the reunification issue and defy the directives of the central authority? To what extent will the preoccupation of the CCP leadership with its internal problems, including the succession crisis, constrain its ability to force Taiwan to accept its political design?

We lack definite answers to these questions, but suffice it to say that it would be better for the consolidation of the new democracy if the issue of reunification were not forced upon Taiwan society early or soon. An aggressive and/or hostile reunification campaign by mainland China would intensify political polarization in Taiwan and put the new regime under severe stress. New democracy needs some breathing space that can be created by the development of a constructive bilateral relationship with mainland China and a congenial international economic environment.

Lastly, the trend of Taiwan's domestic socioeconomic development will have important consequences. By the year 2000, more than 80 percent of the voters will be born in postwar years, will have received a good education, enjoyed the unprecedented level of economic affluence, and shared more common background than their elders regardless of ethnic origin. Many will be cosmopolitan in outlook, sophisticated and articulate. We have reason to believe that the ideological orientation of this electorate will be predominantly centralist, constraining both the maximalist strategy of the opposition camp and reactionary tendencies in the KMT.

Equally important is the degree of popular support and allegiance of this postwar generation to the new democracy. How will they evaluate the performance of the new party system, electoral politics, and representative institutions? Will they unequivocally embrace the democratic ideal and vigorously defend this new system, or will their support for the new regime be a conditional one, depending on the efficiency, responsiveness, and cleanliness of the new regime and quality of public policies? If they have unreasonably high expectations of democratic institutions they could easily become disillusioned. This is not implausible because the KMT's past success in steering economic development and social transformation could create a kind of lingering nostalgia among the populace for the "order and purposeful efficiency" they experienced at the zenith of KMT rule. It is no accident that the so-called "Hau Pei-tsun phenomenon" can happen despite the general trend toward democracy. There is evidence that Taiwan's recent social disorder and recurring violent confrontation in the streets and in the parliament worry many businessmen and ordinary citizens, and that this turmoil and confusion is often attributed to the unruly and ungovernable nature of democracy. The fact that the emerging new regime inherits a record of successful economic development has a double-edged implication for the consolidation of the new democracy. On the one hand, the new regime will be not be overloaded with insurmountable economic difficulties. On the other hand, the old regime will not be totally discredited, and thus will remain a viable alternative.

There are growing concerns among leaders of social movements and middle-class–based interest groups that the new democracy might not serve their interests well. Under the existing electoral arrangements and campaign practices, local factions and big business are well positioned to capture the newly opened electoral arena and representative institutions. As a result, the quality of public policies and autonomy of the state bureaucracy might suffer from the relentless pursuit of economic or political favors, a kind of structured corruption now prevailing in local politics. If that happens, the societal momentum for far-reaching democratic reform might gradually run out of steam.

In addition to these three kinds of structural constraints, some dynamic factors are also involved. The most important is the contingent nature of regime transition itself. For Taiwan, democratization will not be complete without a fundamental realignment of the state-civil society relationship and consequently a clear separation of the party and the state. It also will not be complete without the depoliticization of the military-security apparatus which has been an integral part of the authoritarian ruling coalition. On its way to full democracy, Taiwan must muddle through a number of important junctures which could turn out to be impassable bottlenecks. This depends on not only the shifting preferences and expectations of the electorate, but also the realignment of the power structure within the KMT and interactions between the incumbent elite and the opposition. Their strategic decisions and even their perception of the situation and interests carry significant weight in determining the outcome.

To predict the outcome of regime transition, we need to probe four crucial questions. The first is whether the KMT and the opposition, essentially the DPP, can eventually strike a grand compromise on the issues of constitutional reform and national identity. At this moment there seem many barriers to compromise. Does this mean it may be necessary to wait for a whole generation of the old leadership in the two camps to pass away before more pragmatic elements arrive on the scene with more innovative and accommodating strategies? The second question is whether the reformist leaders in the ruling coalition have the necessary skills and resources to balance conflicting demands and cross pressures coming from all sides. Can they marginalize the hard-liners or the conservative bloc within the KMT? If not, it will be very difficult for the reform-minded leadership to consolidate democracy.

Third, we have to ask how the military and the security apparatus will reposition itself in response to the seemingly irreversible trend toward democracy. Are they willing to return to their barracks, stay above partisan politics, subject themselves to civilian authority and parliamentary supervision, and not claim any special prerogatives in internal security affairs? Or are they going to involve themselves even more actively in party politics and electoral politics to secure their existing prerogatives? The prospect of depoliticization is not very good because the military is by nature a highly exclusive and hierarchical organization. It is very difficult to precipitate significant reorientation or rapid personnel turnover in the military apparatus from the outside.

Lastly, we need to raise the question about the resolve and the willingness of the emerging indigenous elite in the KMT to carry out thorough democratic reform. There can be little doubt that they are the major beneficiary of both the Taiwanization policy and the recent democratic reforms. But it is doubtful that they will remain strong supporters of further democratization once they control the commanding height of the Kuomintang and the state apparatus. It is not inconceivable that they might defend the prerogatives of the ruling party just as adamantly as the old guard did. They might refuse to make concession to the opposition for relinquishing their partisan control over the education system, mass media, associational organizations, and the judicial branch, much less KMT's coveted ownership of privileged business operation and monopolistic enterprises. They might prefer an indigenized authoritarian system to a fully democratic one. On this score, there is little ground for optimism.

There are few other societies where the future seems so uncertain, so open-ended. People cite many analogies: East and West Germany in terms of reunification, Spain in terms of democratic transition, Cyprus for protracted polarized ethnic conflict and external intervention. But none of these seem appropriate. For my part, I think what will most likely emerge from the transition is a hybrid, a hybrid of authoritarian design and representative democracy. On the one hand, the KMT will be transformed and further indigenized. Taiwan's future political system may conform to many objective criteria for liberal democracy. There will be regular elections to decide which party is going to control the government. You will have some genuine competitiveness in electoral politics. Personal freedom will be better protected from the arbitrary acts of the state agencies. On the other hand, the KMT will confine the scope of democratic reform to what Terry Karl has termed "electoralism." The abundant institutional and ideological resources the incumbent elite now enjoys will enable them to resist certain changes that might seriously undermine their power base. The DPP may end up being a permanent opposition, much like the Socialist Party in Japan, with no realistic chance of being in power. The KMT may well continue to maintain its electoral dominance and close institutional links with all major social sectors. The military and security apparatus will continue to be politicized and to enjoy prerogatives absent in a true democracy. There will continue to be partisan control of the mass media, the bureaucracy, the education system, and even the judicial system. In sum, there will still be some strong authoritarian residuals in the new regime. This means Taiwan will be moving toward a political system that lies between Mexico and Japan today. In other words, the momentum of democratization will be checked by forces of inertia, yielding both continuity and discontinuity.

Antonio Chiang
As a reporter for the past twenty years, I've become very skeptical about politics and also about politicians. At the moment, it seems difficult, even impossible, to predict the future in the year 2000. Who would have guessed what happened in Eastern Europe? Or what has happened in Taiwan? Everything changed so much, so quickly. So I do not dare to predict what will happen in the year 2000. But I want to share with you my

personal observations of what a reporter saw happening in politics in the past two years.

I saw the politicians change their color easily, all at once and in both parties. Now everybody loves democracy. I remember a few years ago that many scholars and politicians were strong defenders of martial law, but now they are champions of democracy.

I saw political prisoners suddenly become the most important guests of the KMT and hold closed-door meetings. I saw Chinmen opened for secret negotiations between high-ranking Communist officials and our generals there. I saw Taiwan delegations at the Asian Development Bank meeting and the Asian Games.

I saw the DPP and KMT change their positions. Some DPP members now are more KMT than the KMT. Some KMT members are more an opposition than the DPP and the DPP is much more anti-Communist than the KMT.

Everyone knows that the chairman of the KMT was criticized bitterly by high-ranking officials in his own party. Although Chiang Ching-kuo was reluctant to entrust his close associate Hau Pei-tsun with undisputed control of the military, now suddenly he has become our premier. That's a startling episode.

With such a surprising past, how can I dare predict what will happen in the year 2000? I prefer to provide some personal observations.

I will start with Hau Pei-tsun. I don't believe that kind of political marriage will have a good ending. He and Lee Teng-hui come from two different worlds. Hau is like a Black Knight for Lee Teng-hui, as an exterminator of chaos. His popularity rises every day. Perhaps that is because at the beginning people expected so little of him. From the time he was appointed until now there have not been any serious demonstrations, and so in that way he has maintained order. But I can foresee that if one day they had a real demonstration, Hau would want to use force and there would be a serious confrontation. When I said Hau Pei-tsun and Lee Teng-hui come from different worlds, it's because they have nothing in common. In his heart, Lee is a Taiwanese. By temperament, he's Japanese. He has American ideas. And he was put into the emperor's clothes. People can see that Lee Teng-hui is a man of culture. He likes to go to concerts, likes classical music Hau Pei-tsun likes to go to Peking opera, which Lee Teng-hui does not understand at all.

People in Taiwan will claim that Taiwanese opera is very similar to Peking opera. But no Taiwanese is able to become an actor in Peking opera, because it's very sophisticated, very artful. The use of the movement of eyes, small delicate gestures. The Taiwanese don't know how to behave in this way. That's why Lee Teng-hui had to choose Hau Pei-tsun, because he is a military man and quite straightforward. Lee Teng-hui had very bad relations with Li Huan because Li Huan is a product of the kind of politics Lee understands very little and, I think, doesn't like.

Fortunately or maybe unfortunately, through a historical accident, Lee Teng-hui became chairman of a party he didn't know particularly well, a party he didn't like most of his life. He had had nothing to do with the party. He had no party credentials. That's why he has so many problems with the party. That's why he's so isolated. He doesn't know how to use the party machine. He's a man who doesn't know much about Chinese tradition, Chinese culture, Chinese philosophy. Maybe he will now try to learn about it. He had strong enough lessons in a very short time, just three months. Last March the power struggle almost scared him to death. He was quite isolated. The only thing he could do is pray. Luckily, he has a god to pray to.

Lee Teng-hui is the chairman of the Kuomintang, and he understands that democratization in Taiwan entails the need to transform his party quickly and drastically. He has to make the Chinese Kuomintang into a Taiwanese Kuomintang. Not only that, he has to make an authoritarian party into a democratic party.

The KMT is not really a Leninist party. The party machinery does not function very effectively. Party officials don't make decisions. For the past forty years it has been one man's party. Now no one is in charge. The chairman and the secretary general of the party are both outsiders. Now if the president wants to change the party, he has to bring in new blood, so he is recruiting parliamentarians and scholars. It is a difficult job because he needs the support of the party in order to dismantle the authoritarian part of the party. This is why he has such serious problems in party control.

The party reform plan drafted last year by James Soong has been put on the shelf because of strong resistance from party cadres. So the struggle to transform the KMT from an authoritarian party to a democratic party is difficult and dangerous. Now a lot of people inside the party advocate internal democracy. But James Soong as secretary general and Lee Teng-hui as the chairman regard that kind of demand for internal democracy as only a pretext and a part of the power struggle. It is the professional party officeholders who are demanding "internal democracy." They can easily control the party machine. Those demanding internal democracy inside the party in fact do not want to see the KMT as a democratic party. They want the party rules to be more democratic so they can get power. Those who advocate democracy inside the party are opposed to direct election of the state president and to democracy outside the party.

There is another hot issue now in Taiwan, the National Unification Commission. The question of unification and independence is the most important issue facing Taiwan. But I think many people understand that the real purpose of the Unification Commission established by the president is not the reunification of China, it's the unification of the KMT. That's much more important than the unification of China.

Perhaps they want to keep an option for unification in the future. But unification is not even a long-term plan, it's no plan at all, it's only a dream, or to some people a nightmare. That's why the DPP adopted a resolution on Taiwan's de facto sovereignty. When the people talk about how they feel about unification, they talk about how they fear the Communists. They don't really want to unify with them. Unification is beyond everybody's imagination. Nobody is really thinking about practical steps toward unification. Lee's idea in creating this commission is to dissipate conservative criticism. People have criticized him for working for an independent Taiwan, and he wants to stop that kind of criticism. Lee wants to baptize the KMT in "unification" just like Christians are baptized in their religion. Once you are baptized you can go to school, get all kinds of jobs, and it doesn't matter. As long as you are baptized, you are a Christian. That is the real mission of the Unification Commission. But we also understand that independence is a very difficult question. Not only because of the past forty years of indoctrination by China-orientated education but for many other reasons as well, including ideological problems. In addition, the policy of allowing people so much contact with China will make things much more complicated in the future. The politicians, businessmen, media, artists, writers, all have a stake on mainland China now, so it will be difficult to have a consensus in the future. Because of these visits, the Taiwanese are now more knowledgeable about the mainland than the mainlanders. The mainlanders' memory of the mainland is not as important as the recent experience of Taiwanese people, especially Taiwanese businessmen. This will affect our image of and policies toward the mainland in the future.

I expect that political contact between Taipei and Beijing will begin only after the old generation of leadership in Beijing fades away. When these people fade away, the civil war mentality will fade away. Then leaders on both sides can be more practical. In that way they can create more reasonable relations. As long as the old guard there in Beijing still holds power, I don't a see real possibility of more political contacts. But I expect the old guard in Beijing cannot last much longer.

There is quite a lot we can do between the two poles of unification or independence. The KMT says that without unification we have no real democracy, and the DPP says that without independence we have no chance of democracy. The two parties use this in their power struggle. Without democracy we can never create a consensus in Taiwan. Without consensus we can go neither to unification nor to independence, for if a substantial part of the population is opposed, there can be no movement. So before anybody can decide the Taiwanese future there needs to be a basic consensus. Consensus has to come first. Nobody can expect that another declaration of martial law, another wave of arrests putting dissidents in jail will make independence or unification possible. The mainlanders and the Taiwanese are hostage to each other. We are in the same boat. Everybody has a veto, so don't worry about the shouting or the political slogans.

As a reporter I think the KMT should do much more to implement democracy. Lee Teng-hui has said that direct election of the president will lose us legitimacy as the representatives of China. That kind of talk will only escalate a confrontation with the independence movement. That kind of talk leads to challenges and escalation, a kind of confrontation bad for Taiwan.

Cheng Hsing-ti
I am both Professor of Political Science of the National Chengchi University and Deputy Director of the Department of Social Affairs of the KMT party. But since my duties at the Department of Social Affairs have nothing to do with constitutional reform,

I would like to speak on today's topic as a professor.

The topic of the panel, Taiwan in the Year 2000, is both compelling and challenging. It is compelling because the decision maker can steer the course of the nation. And it is challenging because making predictions of future events is a risky exercise. In this short presentation, I will use scenario planning as did Professor Chu Yun-han earlier. Scenario planning is a technique developed by Professor Pierre Wack of the Harvard Business School. It is used to examine alternative plans for the future of certain political cultures or social events. Scenario planning, according to Professor Wack, can effectively organize a variety of seemingly unrelated political, social, and economic information and translate it into a framework for judgment. I will first try to map out the political ecology that will set the stage for electoral competition among political parties in Taiwan.

At the National Affairs Conference, one of the task forces working on constitutional reform proposed changes in the provincial and municipal administrative structure. There were three propositions concerning the remodeling of local government. Proposition One favored multiple provinces and multiple municipalities. Proposition Two recommended one province and multiple municipalities. Proposition Three suggested one province and three municipalities. At the moment, the Ministry of the Interior tends to favor the third proposition. If it is finally accepted, the future political ecology of the island will be composed of one province, plus three large municipalities, so-called special cities, instead of the current one province and two municipalities. The National Affairs Conference recommended that the provincial governor and the mayors of the special cities be elected by popular vote in the future.

Another parameter of political ecology will be the changing structure of the Legislative Yuan. After the retirement of senior parliamentarians by the end of 1991, voters in Taiwan will elect a total of 150 new members to the Legislative Yuan in 1992. I believe the KMT will continue to retain a majority of the votes in future local, provincial, and national elections. However, with seven county magistrates and city mayors already controlled by DPP and independent politicians, plus twenty-one opposition members in the current Legislative Yuan, if they continue to capture additional seats in the three special cities and forty more seats in the legislative body, they could pose a severe threat to the continuation of KMT rule.

If the DPP succeeds in its strategy to "encircle" the central government by electoral victories at the local level, it might then demand the creation of a grand governing coalition of KMT, DPP, and independent politicians. In fact, two non-KMT members were named to cabinet posts in June 1990.

In addition to the two parameters of political ecology on the domestic scene, a third parameter concerns the future interaction between the two rival regimes across the Taiwan Straits. The KMT, harboring an unfulfilled historic mission and also contending with growing pressure both from the DPP and overseas Taiwanese advocating a pro-independence stand, could opt for reconciliation and rapprochement with the Communist regime of mainland China. A scenario could be written in the following fashion.

In Stage One, with the infusion of capital investment and technological know-how by the Beijing government and by private and semi-official sectors across the Taiwan Straits, the coastal provinces of Guangdong, Hainan, and Fujian, plus the economic powerhouses of Hong Kong and Taiwan, become a growth triangle igniting economic achievement throughout Southeastern China in the coming decade.

Stage Two, the impetus of Southeastern China's economic power and the introduction of a market economy by the Soviet Union would eventually force the Chinese Communist government to abandon its central planning system and initiate economic pluralization.

Stage Three, economic pluralization spills over to the realm of political life.

Stage Four, political democratization on the mainland encourages the Nationalist Chinese government on Taiwan to open a dialogue with the Communist government. A KMT mini-Marshall Plan would be launched to promote further economic development on the mainland.

Stage Five, a system transformation process takes place on the mainland and the two societies across the Taiwan Straits converge.

Stage Six, a loose format of political linkages is established between the two political entities. The future relationship between mainland China and Taiwan would be similar to that of Denmark and Greenland. In principle, I believe there would be a high degree of autonomy for the island province to run its own internal affairs, with Taiwan also taking care of its foreign and international matters. In addition, an Executive Council with a power-sharing mechanism would be formed to protect the vital interests of the island's population and to make decisions on matters of common interest across the Taiwan Straits.

This is a scenario and a system that I believe will fit the way of life for 1.1 billion Chinese people on both sides of the Taiwan Straits.

Chin Sheng-pao

The first Spanish words I learned were, "Que Sera, Sera." The future is not ours to see, but we can guess.

The problem that most concerns the people of Taiwan is the question of unification or independence. I would like to point to some basic factors that will influence this question. First is the changing structure of the population. Right now, people born after 1949 constitute 70 percent of the population. By the end of this decade the percentage will be 80 to 85. Most of the younger generation, therefore, will have no sentimental feeling toward the mainland, whether their parents come from mainland China or not.

The second factor is democratization. As the political parties become more democratic, they move further toward indigenization. Politicians will want to appeal to the indigenous people by talking about indigenous issues of concern, not Taiwanese or mainlander issues. As a result of this process, unification will have less and less appeal.

There will also be the examples of the incorporation of Hong Kong and Macau into mainland China, Hong Kong in 1997 and Macau in 1999. From historical experience, this form of return of colonies to the motherland usually causes some unrest and disturbance. That unrest and disturbance will strengthen the view on Taiwan to resist the unification with the mainland.

There is a growing feeling of isolation among people in Taiwan. The lack of formal recognition of the ROC by the international community is likely to persist. We know that support for separation is strongest among those who are more educated, and have had more trips abroad. If international isolation persists, that will enhance the popular feeling to try to break out of this isolation by declaring independence.

Factors are also likely to emerge in mainland China to influence its stance on unification. There will be a new leadership in Beijing. We don't know who will be in power in the late 1990s. But the new leadership for its own reasons may have to take a stronger position on forceful unification. The return of Hong Kong and Macau may make them over-confident of their ability to unify China. Taiwan is their main target.

Unification and independence are the two extreme possibilities. I have an alternative view on the future. First, during the 1990s greater understanding will develop between the people of mainland China and the island China of Taiwan. More and more people from Taiwan will have visited the mainland, and will have formed their own impression of the mainland. Not necessarily a good impression, but a good understanding. They will have developed some sort of a friendly feeling toward the people in the mainland, though not necessarily toward the regime in Beijing. Over the years, that feeling can be developed, and they will feel less the necessity for independence from China.

Secondly, there will be greater admiration of Taiwan by the people of the mainland. Those travelling to mainland China already have seen that people, especially the common people, feel that Taiwan is richer and more stable and also free. That will make it more difficult for the regime in Beijing, whether Communist or non-Communist, to use force to solve the unification problem.

Last, there will be a large number of bright young people from both sides of the Taiwan Straits who have been educated in Western countries. They will constitute the mainstream of both societies. The first group of students from mainland China studying in the U.S. started in about 1980. At that time, let us say they were on average twenty years old. They encountered Taiwan students on Western campuses, and studied together with them. This has developed a better understanding between them. By the year 2000, this group will be forty years old, and becoming more prominent.

Investment and trade from Taiwan will also create a kind of bonding between the business circles in Taiwan and those in the mainland. This will help solve the unification problem in a peaceful way. The progress of democracy all over the world is also favorable to the ROC in its competition with the PRC. As many of my colleagues have pointed out, democracy is the only way to solve the China problem.

In conclusion, I believe the separate and independent development of Taiwan and the mainland will continue, but the distance between the two paradigms will become closer rather than wider as some people predict. They probably will not merge into one. That means the status quo will still exist in the year 2000. The two lines will come closer and closer. Eventually they will meet. But not in this century.

Parris Chang

Politics is a struggle to determine who gets what, when and how. If we use that definition of politics to look at Taiwan's future, there are many issues to be analyzed.

We can ask, who participates? With what kind of perspective? Through what kind of control, or commanding what resources? Using what kind of strategy, and wishing for what kind of outcome?

We know that there is an ongoing process of political democratization bringing more Taiwanese into the political arena. Farmers, workers, housewives, consumers, environmentalists, the political opposition, and many other protest groups are taking part in politics. They lobby in the legislature, hold mass rallies, and court media attention to publicize their cause. The arena and channels of participation are also expanding and changing.

In so far as participants are concerned, they are not confined only to those in Taiwan. We find that Beijing has become increasingly more involved in the political process in Taiwan. This past March, during the presidential election in Taiwan, Beijing issued a pointed statement and sought to intervene against president Lee Teng-hui, but to no avail. Some KMT politicians in Taiwan have tried to "play the China card" by having liaisons with the Communists on the mainland. We will see change in the "rules of the game" and expansions in the "arena of conflict" in Taiwan as time goes on because those mainlander politicians who feel they are in the minority in Taiwan certainly are going to invoke the support of Beijing to redress the balance.

I believe that as time goes by, the KMT is going to get less than 60 percent of the votes, and scoring less than 50 percent of the votes is a possibility. Thus, for the KMT to lose political power is no longer unthinkable, but that depends on whether or not the DPP can get its act together and mobilize enough popular support. It is often pointed out that the DPP is divided into factions, but this should not be exaggerated. Factionalism and disunity is not the sole prerogative of the DPP. We have witnessed much of the same thing in the KMT in the past seven months. So between the KMT and the DPP, it's not just balance of power. There is also a balance of weakness. The side making fewer mistakes is going to win in the future.

The relationship between state and society is changing in important ways. In the past, the KMT, whether a personal dictatorship or a Leninist party, was able to control virtually every area of social and political life, and exhibited considerable ability to mobilize support for its policy. Clearly the KMT is fast losing this capability to control and mobilize, not only because of the loss of its strong man, but loss of other elements of power (e.g., legitimacy) as well. Pluralistic tendencies are growing, and there is no longer only one center of power. The state has to deal with economic and social groups and treat their input seriously.

As time goes by, neither the KMT nor the executive branch can continue to dominate the legislature, ordering it to do this and do that at will. Conflict between party apparatchiki and those in the legislature (and those in the government) is already evident. The relationship between the ruling party and government officials is changing, as is the relationship between the executive and the legislature. Until now, the executive branch dominated the legislature. Increasingly, the executive branch is going to have to take more advice from the legislators and consult more. It will have to set up a consultation mechanism to get the input of the legislative branch. This change is already evident. Within the executive branch, it is no longer the president who calls the shots. The president and the prime minister have to work out a kind of modus vivendi because until now the power relationship between the two has not been institutionalized but instead has been based on personality.

As all these factors change, three alternatives for Taiwan's future in the post-Chiang era hang in the balance: democracy, autocracy, or chaos. One very important issue that could affect Taiwan's future is its relationship with the PRC. As stated earlier, within the KMT some people have tried to play the "China card." They are mostly mainlander members of the National Assembly and the Legislative Yuan; they are in their seventies and eighties and still they try to hang on to their positions of power, and resist or slow the pace of democratization, and this is rather troublesome.

I find the scenario proposed by Professor Cheng Hsing-ti interesting, it could have been written by someone in Zhao Ziyang's brain trust. I don't know whether people in Taiwan and our friends in the DPP would necessarily favor this kind of scenario, because it looks like more the perspective of the mainlanders.

We cannot overlook, indeed we cannot emphasize enough, the importance of identity in Taiwan's politics. Those who were born in Taiwan and those who were born in the mainland who came to Taiwan after 1949 have very different visions of Taiwan's future and how democratization ought to be implemented. The mainlanders place emphasis on unification with the mainland, the Taiwanese prefer independence. Many Taiwanese feel that the mainlanders have been using the question of unification to block Taiwan's political reform and democratization, and it provokes them to go to extremes and call for Taiwan's independence.

In my own analysis of Taiwan's relations with the mainland, I see 1997 will be troublesome because Hong Kong will come under PRC control that year. We can expect Beijing to intensify the campaign for unification with Taiwan before 1997, putting a lot of pressure on Taiwan to come to the negotiating table. Conceivably the old guard, the political dinosaurs in Beijing, if they haven't died by 1997, will certainly try very hard to have some kind of result before they go. How well the leadership and the people in Taiwan respond to and resist the forthcoming pressure will be very crucial.

Nevertheless, I agree with several speakers who have stated that the relations between Taiwan and the mainland in the long term will become smoother. With the civil war generation out of the picture, the leaderships in both Taipei and Beijing will be more pragmatic, more rational, and they could work out some kind of modus vivendi. Unification is not a foregone conclusion. Whether the outcome is going to be "two nations, two systems," or a loose confederation or some kind of a commonwealth under the name of China, is an open-ended question.

Given their long history of hostility, enmity, and continued distrust, and that the two societies have differed so much in their ways of life and value systems (not to mention differences in political and economic systems), the situation is such that one cannot put Humpty Dumpty back together again. Therefore, it is unrealistic to talk about peaceful unification. The more practical issue is whether the two sides can work out some kind of modus vivendi so that both can benefit from growing interactions and expanding cultural and economic ties.

Andrew J. Nathan
I would like to comment on what we have heard this afternoon from what I imagine to be the perspective of a policymaker in Beijing. Coming into the conference, I would have held four beliefs. First, I would believe that at the present time compromise on the status of Taiwan is for me politically impossible. If I start to make compromises on Taiwan, other politicians will attack me. Second, I would believe that although the U.S. says, "We really have no policy on the Taiwan

question, we just want a peaceful resolution," in fact they do have a policy and it is to prevent me from extending my control over Taiwan. Third, I would believe that the moderate DPP and moderate KMT forces are cooperating to achieve the so-called *kuo-tu*, or independence, without the explicit declaration of a break in constitutional continuity, doing everything they can to firm up the island's survivability as an entity outside mainland control. Finally, I would believe that only a tough, uncompromising line has any hope of arresting these trends. Therefore we must continuously work to cut off all of Taiwan's other options and wait until Taiwan's residents have no other choice but to align with us.

At this conference, I have learned some things, although I'm not sure that any of these conclusions are what people really meant to say.

First, I get the impression that, as Chang Chün-hung said, there's nobody in control. The government is weak. Prior to today's meeting, I had the impression that Lee Teng-hui had seized the initiative when the students demonstrated at the Chiang Kai-shek Memorial Hall, that he had taken that opportunity to strengthen his position in the KMT, and to push forward reform. But in today's discussion, I got the impression Lee Teng-hui is on the defensive, that the push is coming from the opposition and the people. Although some of our panelists suggested that the security forces are in control, they have not been able to prevent the DPP from adopting a resolution that Taiwan's actual sovereignty does not extend to the mainland. As a mainland official, I would be very concerned about the government's apparent weakness.

The second thing I would notice is that the opposition has been able to shift the ground of debate on Taiwan's status. First, the National Affairs Conference reaches a consensus that the well-being and security of the residents of Taiwan should be the basic premise for national policy, which is a dangerous premise from the viewpoint of the mainland authorities. If Taiwan is merely one small province in a great nation, you can't make its residents' welfare the primary basis of policy, and any policy that's based on that premise is going to be a bad policy for unification.

Third, I discover that Columbia University organizes a conference and tries to be very balanced, yet we hear from no one who predicts or desires anything like the realization of the mainland's policy.

The reforms that are taking place all go in the direction of making the Taiwan political system look more and more like a self-contained and integral state. It's going to become a place where the elected representatives primarily represent the people who live there, and where the chief executive is elected by the people who live there. Then we hear that there's consideration of making more than one province within Taiwan. All this makes it look more like a self-sufficient entity. Then we hear Professor Cheng predicting one of the most "optimistic" scenarios for unification. What he says is that we will have unification after the mainland gives up its entire economic and political system and becomes a virtual extension of the Taiwan political and economic system. At that point Taiwan will consider a loose confederation in which the mainland has no real power over Taiwan.

All this suggests that the National Affairs Conference crystallized a series of trends in which things are getting worse for me as a mainland policymaker. What am I going to do about it? I look at my options. I could attack militarily. But I'm not confident that my military machine will be able to chug across the Straits. And I'm concerned about the impact of an attack on my international standing, so I drop the idea. I could mount a boycott and, as David Dean said, push up the price of maritime insurance to strangle Taiwan's commerce, but again I'm worried about the impact of this on my modernization program. I could smuggle guns from Xiamen and hope that social order in Taiwan falls apart, but I'm already doing this and it hasn't had that deep an effect. I could flood Taiwan with immigrants, but on the other hand they have already met with me on Chinmen to make plans to send them all back. I could invite the Taiwan capitalists to come and invest, and then when I have them all here I could squeeze them. The trouble is, they're coming over here and having a very hard time making money. The wave of Taiwan investment is rather slow. So what you seem to have is a situation in which the mainland doesn't have any appetizing options, and is just watching Taiwan float away.

Is there any reason to think that the mainland will change their policy? Parris Chang gave some reasons why the mainland could change, including generational change in the leadership. But we don't see any signs yet that change is in the works. It's a rational scenario, but not yet an empirical reality.

Is it possible for the Taiwan side of the picture to change? Again, some scenarios have been suggested. Chang Chün-hung says that he's afraid that the Taiwan economic situation might get much worse, or that there could be a violent revolution. David Dean was concerned that if there were a declaration of independence, it would worsen Taiwan's diplomatic situation. But such doomsday scenarios seem to be fairly unlikely. And their consequences would not necessarily be conducive to unification. So as a mainland official, I would come away with a murky and not very optimistic picture.

Chi Su
Before going into the international aspects of Taiwan's situation, I would like to suggest that some of the comments heard here today were exaggerated. For instance, Professor Parris Chang, whom I admire, has exaggerated the importance of the role of ethnicity in Taiwan. From Beijing's point of view, both mainlanders and Taiwanese are considered Taiwanese. On the

other hand, Professor Cheng Hsing-ti's scenario for long-term reunification seems to be over-optimistic. Taiwan, although richer and more powerful than before, is not going to have that kind of impact on the mainland.

Thinking about the foreign relations of Taiwan, I would like to delineate three sets of factors. The first set concerns the PRC factor which will continue to be the most important one affecting Taiwan's foreign relations in the future. There are several elements of PRC policy to which we should pay close attention. First, the PRC has begun paying greater attention to Taiwan affairs recently and perhaps will continue to do so in the near future. You probably have heard of or seen the interview recently given by Yang Shangkun to *China Times* Editor-in-Chief Huang Chao-sung. Reliable sources told us that after Yang's aide gave him a copy of the *China Times*, he spent two hours reading the published report while his aide stood by. But I am not confident that the PRC leadership, especially the "eight elderly venerables," read the situation in Taiwan as we read it. I think there is a high chance that they misunderstand the situation in Taiwan despite the fact that their analysts on the working level are better informed of our situation than before. I get the feeling that they constantly blame the big guys for the troubles in the little guys. They blame the Soviet Union for the troubles in Eastern Europe. They blame the United States for the Taiwan situation. They blame the KMT for the misbehavior of the DPP. This seems a constant misperception. Maybe it is just propaganda, but I think to some degree it reflects what they really think.

Second, the PRC is trying to build a web of interest and personal relations on Taiwan to nurture a coalition of pro-PRC interest groups in order to affect Taiwan's mainland policy in the future. This has been going on since November 1987, when the ban on visiting the mainland was lifted.

The third element of PRC policy is that they will continue to insist on the "one country, two systems" formula. This formula is ambiguous on some crucial points. For instance, to the best of my knowledge, they haven't clarified their stand on arms sales for Taiwan. If China is to be unified under this formula, can Taiwan continue to get arms from the United States or other countries? Or can we only get water guns, toy pistols? Also, what kind of relations can Taiwan have with the rest of the world? It is not clear whether and to what extent we can participate in bilateral or multilateral international forums. These considerations are important omissions from the PRC's formula.

The fourth element of the PRC's Taiwan policy is the effort to isolate Taiwan internationally. The fifth is that the PRC has never renounced the use of force on the pretext of reducing the incentive to certain foreign countries to intervene in Taiwan. Thus far the PRC has never named these foreign countries, but recent PRC publications have constantly used U.S.-Panama and U.S.-Grenada as targets of denunciation, so I think there is no doubt about who that "foreign country" is.

These are the five elements of the PRC's policy toward Taiwan, and I think they will continue as long as the current leadership lives. PRC policy is and will continue to be a kind of imperial rhetoric, full of sweet talk and empty promises, while exerting pressure on us from all sides. Some people in Taiwan may be for unification, some for independence. But the reality is that as long as the PRC insists on no independence, there will be no independence. I respect people who spend years advocating certain causes. But I'm afraid as realists, we have to face reality, that is, the existence of the PRC and its hegemonistic policy toward Taiwan.

The second set of factors affecting Taiwan's foreign policy is the international situation, which seems to me more favorable than the probable course of development of PRC policy. There is a favorable part and an unfavorable part. The unfavorable part, which I'll mention first, is that the PRC now has normalized relations with the Soviet Union and India, and relations are improving with Vietnam, South Korea, and all the neighbors. Although, as Ambassador Dean said, the PRC is preoccupied with all sorts of domestic problems, the improvement of its international relations gives the PRC a free hand to pursue unification, and the Taiwan issue is now higher on their agenda. From Taiwan's point of view, we hope that they will look the other way, but unfortunately they are looking straight at us.

On the other hand, the international situation is also developing in our favor. The PRC likes to say that there are two major trends in the world: development and peace. Actually, there is also a third, democratization. And Taiwan is moving along with all three trends. If Taiwan continues to democratize itself, as we are doing now despite all of the debate over details and processes, and as long as we hold on to our economic miracle and refrain from making trouble in the international arena, I think we will make more and more friends in the future despite PRC pressure.

The third major factor is our own politics and policy—a difficult question to analyze. It would take a whole conference to do that. But generally speaking, whoever is in power, whichever faction, whichever party, I think that in the future our foreign policy will continue to be flexible and pragmatic. I don't think the rigidity of the past is going to return.

One should not get too jittery about superficial phenomena. People talk about the resolution passed by the DPP on the initiative of Mr. Yao Chia-wen, which said that the national sovereignty of the ROC does not extend to the mainland. Professor Winckler mentioned that Premier Hau's authority was invoked to try to stop the passing of this resolution. But I think from a *realpolitik* point of view, it was good politics. The passing of this resolution serves to signal to the PRC that some people in Taiwan are thinking about independence, not unification as Beijing likes to presume. But at the same time, the premier's action serves to signal to the PRC that the KMT government is still in control. This is the kind of balancing act that we constantly have to do, balancing between the unification force and the independence force. I think in the future the ROC will continue to survive and develop in the international arena, but it takes careful management. Prudence and patience are required. Single-minded advocacy of a particular cause is not going to benefit us.

I am reminded of an American saying, "The best is the enemy of the good." If you're looking only for an ideal, either unification or independence, you may find you can get neither. Good intentions often lead us nowhere. So this is what we face now and are going to face in the future. There is no easy or quick solution. We have to be patient and prudent.

Paul S.P. Hsu

I share the confusion mentioned by Andrew Nathan and Professor Su. I see a cartoon in front of me. Different parties are holding each other by the neck, but gently enough not to strangle each other, and once in a while they wink at each other. At first I thought there were only three parties, the Communist party, the KMT, and the DPP, but now I think I was wrong. There would be at least two factions in the DPP, two factions in the KMT, and I don't know how many factions in the Chinese Communist Party. You see by the cartoon that there is an impasse. Under such an impasse, there can be no quick solution.

I was instructed to talk about economic implications. When we talk about economic implications, we cannot leave out the private business sector. They traditionally have been looked down upon by academic circles and government officials. "They are only looking after profit, they have no ideas." But they are normal people of flesh and blood. They like the arts, they like music, and they're concerned about the future.

Suddenly in the past couple of years they have been invited by every politician, including President Lee Teng-hui, ex-premier Li Huan, and the current premier, Hau Pei-tsun, to dinner. I'm sure they're being invited by DPP leaders, too. And at those occasions, each is given two, three, or maybe five minutes to say something. After that nothing much happens except that they are asked to make donations; donations to different candidates for different types of elections. And some ex-politician or frustrated politician says, "I want to form a foundation, please donate."

So the businessmen were confused. But they have a strong survival instinct. How do they survive? I cannot represent each of them, but let me try to reflect a few things.

They pretty much feel the government wants to interfere in their business decisions, and that the laws and regulations are outmoded. When new laws and regulations are discussed they have little chance to voice their concern. They feel treated as if they think only about tax evasion. They feel looked upon as people who have no loyalty to the country, who would go anywhere just for survival's sake.

In fact, these are people who are committed to Taiwan. If their business fails, they have nowhere to go. They can emigrate, but they're responsible to many employees. And so what do they think about the political situation? When I ask them, they say things like, "Why can't we have a civil service system? Why can't party politics be independent from day-to-day political administration?"

I agree with them. We need an independent civil service system in Taiwan to install the kind of stability that people require on a day-to-day basis in the administration of public affairs. For most in the private sector, that probably would be their only comment. They might have nothing to say about the political struggle between the KMT and the DPP. Instead, they would turn to their own problems. What are these problems? In

1989 Taiwan still remained a giant economic machine. The trade surplus with the U.S. alone was about $12 billion, down from the $19 billion peak of 1988. When businesspeople heard about the economic miracle in Taiwan, they would say, "Yes, it's truly a miracle under such a bureaucratic system to have such accomplishments." But now they are facing increasing wages. Their wage costs have been increasing faster than productivity. In the last few months, the situation may have been a little better because of the plunge in the stock market. A lot of people are willing to go back to work and take a cut in their salaries.

There are labor problems ranging from labor shortage to labor disputes. This is probably normal from the viewpoint of an American business executive or a European executive, but it's something new to the Taiwan business executive. And environmental problems: waste disposal, air pollution, and so forth. Power shortage problems probably will surface in 1991. There is a serious shortage of industrial land at a reasonable price. In fact, Taiwan probably needs another land reform. There is a problem of outflow of funds because of a lack of investment opportunities in Taiwan. When I say lack of investment opportunity, I'm not talking about the question of expansion or new business operations. I mean they have to compare different investment opportunities and decide whether a particular investment should go to Thailand versus Taiwan, or elsewhere.

Then finally there is inflation.

Now let us look toward the year 2000. We still have this cartoon, with five or seven parties holding each other's necks gently. That means no quick solution to any of those constitutional problems, and debate on the theme of unification versus independence continues. In the absence of a national scale, a far-sighted and forward-looking set of policy guidelines, and a carefully designed government economic policy, the business sector will probably need to resolve corporate strategy themselves. Let's pretend we are all sitting in the boardroom of one of the top one hundred companies in Taiwan. They are thinking about risk, which they have to manage. They are thinking about corporate strategy on a worldwide basis, not just on Taiwan anymore. They are looking constantly for more space, more room for survival and growth. And they have to look around to match their corporate strategies and the future target for growth with what resources are available around them. They have to calculate what resources around them have not been utilized.

With that, I also want to turn to the resources that possibly will still be available toward and beyond the year 2000. If everything goes right under conditions of adequate development of technology, and prudent government policy—which need not be very brilliant, but just prudent enough—and maintenance of the work ethic and social order of a normal kind (I'm not referring to a Utopia), then under such circumstances, I think there will be a continued accumulation of wealth and capital, as reflected in per capita income increase, GNP increase, and foreign exchange reserve increase.

I want to put a qualification on that. When we talk about foreign exchange reserves, we are not talking about counting the chips per se, but are referring to what assets have accumulated on a world scale that are owned by Taiwan companies. In other words, figure the foreign exchange reserve in terms of worldwide assets, including mergers, acquisitions, and creation of new businesses in other parts of the world.

Second, you probably will see continued accumulation of skilled and high quality manpower, following the advancement of the domestic educational system and close cooperation with educational systems and institutions abroad. Now in this regard, I've been toying with the question of whether we need a Ministry of Education at all. How many countries have a Ministry of

Education? Do we need one to enhance our education system? I think overall, the continuing accumulation of skill, training, and high-quality manpower will probably take its natural course. With the accumulation of wealth, there probably will be no problem for the children of the current generation to receive a good education even if the government-sponsored educational system is not good enough.

I would expect to see the continuing internationalization of Taiwan's business sector, resulting in the owning of assets around the world. However, the necessary condition for this is to improve the management of private and government enterprises alike. Prudent government policy is of course vital to the enhancement of the internationalization of Taiwan's business sector and its economy.

International activities of the Taiwan business sector will range from owning and operating business abroad, to joint ventures with world class businesses, to capturing certain niches, such as operating and managing industrial parks around the world. Recently a consortium in Taiwan consisting of five major industries successfully negotiated and will probably put into operation early next year an industrial park in Cork, Ireland. This is, I think a very impressive example of the ability of the private sector to do something on their own in a visionary manner.

Setting up this industrial park in Ireland creates the possibility of being ready for 1992 and the integrated European market. With a certain amount of help from the government, in the next five years they could create another five to ten or twenty industrial parks around the world. Just imagine the implications for Taiwan as a whole!

This is just one example of the continuing internationalization of Taiwan's business sector. I don't think such trends will be stopped by internal political chaos. The private sector with its survival instinct is going to move ahead.

—Floor Discussion—

Chu Yun-han

I want to address the evolving relation between the executive and legislative branches. To appreciate the issue fully, we need to recognize first that for a long time the KMT has retained a duality in its elite recruitment pattern. A duality cuts across the more familiar ethnic division. As a result, the incumbent elite comprises of two distinctive groups—one with a strong electoral base and one relying on the party-state apparatus as its power base. Among the current leadership, you have native politicians like Lee Teng-hui, Chiu Chuang-huan (former head of the Provincial Government), and Shih Chi-yang (deputy prime minister) and the mainlander elite, who climb up the ladder of success mostly through technocratic and/or party posts. They never run in an election, they have no clearly defined constituents, they have no multi-faceted ties to a local community or the social networks in a given locality. On the other hand, you have the so-called election-based politicians who are mostly but not exclusively Taiwanese and try to advance their position in the KMT primarily through their capacity to mobilize electoral resources and deliver an electoral majority that supports the legitimacy of the ruling party. In the past, more state/party-based elite than election-based elite were recruited to the highest echelon of the party and the government because they are more trusted and lack an independent power base outside the party-state hierarchy. Some former electoral politicians, once they were appointed to high-ranking positions, were gradually uprooted from their traditional base and assimilated into the corps of state/party-based elite. Therefore, the election-based elite always plays second fiddle to the state/party-based elite, which comes to dominate the national government and central party organs. However, the election-based elite now has begun asserting itself on the national political scene as they increasingly find the newly opened national representative body a powerful vehicle for upward mobility.

The future evolution of the relation between the executive and legislative branches will necessarily be influenced by this kind of political competition. What kind of executive-legislative relationship is Taiwan likely to have in the future? The best analogy I can think of is what the French Fifth Republic once had. That is, the president of France, in particular Charles De Gaulle and George Pompidou, while being able to maintain a right-wing pro-government majority in the national assembly and controlling the legislative agenda, selected his prime minister and most of his cabinet members from the so called Grand Corps—the elite civil servants and mostly graduates of *grandes écoles*, e.g., ENA (Ecole Nationale d'Administration) or Ecole Polytechnique—rather than from the deputies. They, in turn, tried to limit the influence of partisan politics on the running of the government, and so erected a barrier between the technocrats who dominated the executive branch and the electoral politicians in the legislative arena.

I think for Taiwan this kind of asymmetrical executive-legislative relationship will continue well into the coming decade, provided that the KMT remains in power. The state/party-based elite with the enormous resources at its disposal and the capacity to draw up the rules of party nomination and electoral competition will be able to play one clique against another in the Legislative Yuan and thus effectively break up any coalition among the election-based elite that attempts to challenge their position. This is the reason why the semi-presidential system of the French Fifth Republic is now quite popular among the KMT leadership, who see it as bringing the least disruption to the exiting elite system. Of course, there is a chance that their political fortunes will be reversed if their candidates fail to win the first election for the provincial governor and the mayors of Taipei and Kaohsiung.

Jason C. Hu

Mr. Hong Yuh-Chin asked me to say that the work of the Constitutional Reform Policy Planning Group, whose timetable he gave us this morning, is progressing well. There is a coordination sub-group that is to present these agendas to the political parties so that they can continue in the spirit of the National Affairs Conference. He said that this procedure enables the opposition party to play a supervisory role.

I was much enlightened about the future of Taiwan by the remarks of panelists. We should not forget certain events that we all know are coming up in the near future. We all anticipate the establishment of a Mainland Affairs Commission in the Executive Yuan during the remaining two months of this year. We know that the Ministry of Economic Affairs is taking measures to solve the economic problems that Taiwan is facing today. We know that President Lee Teng-hui said in May 1990 that the Temporary Provisions will be abrogated sometime in 1991. In around May next year perhaps, not only will we see the abrogation of the Temporary Provisions, but we are likely to see the adoption of the bylaws regulating the relationship between Taiwan and mainland China. And after that law is adopted, there will be an intermediary organization dealing with the relationship between both sides of the Taiwan Straits and we also expect to see by the end of 1991 the retirement of all senior parliamentarians who have not previously retired.

You can also foresee that 1992 will be an important election year. The Legislative Yuan will come up for reelection. Many of the county magistrates will come up for reelection. The governor and perhaps the mayors of the special municipalities may come up for reelection.

These events will mean, among other things, a total restructuring of representation in the Legislative Yuan, which would be completely elected by voters in Taiwan and which would no longer include mainland-elected members. The

DPP percentage of the votes may reach 20 or 30 percent, if not more. In 1993, perhaps in February when the new members are sworn in, a new prime minister must be appointed. It may be General Hau, it may not be him. And it will be crucial, I think, to the future development of politics in Taiwan, whether he will or will not be there.

All signs point to the possibility that Hau is already not that closely linked with the military. There are reports saying that a new generation of generals within the army now say that General Hau is a civilian, a prime minister, and he should not meddle in military affairs. That shows the rise of professionalism. It is therefore quite reasonable to assume that in the future there will be less and less military influence in politics in Taiwan.

All these developments will promote the democratization Taiwan and a more important role for the opposition, whoever they may be. I can also foresee that party politics will be more mature, and most of the media will report fairly on the competition.

There is an even more important development coming up in 1996, the presidential election. President Lee has said that he is not going to run. We are reasonably sure that the DPP is going to put forward a candidate to run for presidency in 1996. If we have a National Assembly totally elected by the voters in Taiwan, the DPP would be able to come up with enough support in the Assembly to file for a candidacy. And that would further increase the role an opposition can play in Taiwan's party politics.

But don't forget that by 1996 the intermediary organization dealing with mainland China–Taiwanese relations will have been in existence for five years. By then, there will be more economic, cultural, and other interactions between the two sides. It will be interesting to see whether the new president, whoever he is, will view the relationship between the two sides of the Taiwan Straits with a different perspective once hostility and misunderstanding is reduced.

In short, the future development of politics in Taiwan is bound to include further democratization and a closer relationship across the Taiwan Straits. The closer commercial relationship will be good for businessmen in Taiwan because they can make use of a cheap and stable supply of labor in mainland China. All these factors leave me optimistic about the future economic development of Taiwan, assuming businessmen in Taiwan can adapt to the new situation between two sides of the Taiwan Straits. Finally we can expect the situation to be affected by the personality of the prime minister and the president who will be chosen in the years to come.

Paul S.P. Hsu
I always appreciate optimism and Professor Hu's comments are certainly optimistic. But I would like to hear his comments on the issue of an independent civil service system, and how to remove party politics from the day-to-day administration of government.

Jason C. Hu
If we go on to further democratization, with political parties competing on fair grounds, people will pay attention to concrete policy issues instead of more emotional or radical political issues. This is why I didn't mention a movement for independence. And if you have real party politics, then a neutralization of civil servants becomes possible and you would have a healthy civil service system.

Hung-mao Tien
I have three questions for three panelists. The first is addressed to Professor Chu Yun-han. From my standpoint, political development in Taiwan since 1987 may be conceptualized as a period of rule building, i.e., efforts to rebuild, modify, or

establish ground rules for future democratic politics. I think one of the reasons why the DPP chose to become involved in the National Affairs Conference is because they thought they could influence adoption of new rules that would be beneficial to them. May I ask Professor Chu, how do you think this rule-building process will be completed, and what will be the ground rules affecting the future competition between the KMT and the DPP or other opposition parties?

Second, I echo the view that the year of crisis in the future of Taiwan may not be the year 2000. I think it would be the year 1996 or 1997, not only because Hong Kong will be turned over to the PRC at that time, but also because Taiwan will hold a presidential election. Based on my understanding of Taiwan's political situation, either Lee Teng-hui personally decides not to run for re-election, or will not be allowed to run because of forces within the KMT opposing his bid for another term.

My scenario is that the PRC will try its best to interfere in the domestic political process of Taiwan in the future to make certain that whoever is elected the next president will be someone clearly in favor of unification. If not, drastic steps could be taken to resolve the Taiwan issue. So I would like to ask Professor Cheng, how do you assess the PRC's current plans? Do you agree with my assessment that the PRC is planning an all-out infiltration or involvement in Taiwan's domestic political process in an effort to capture the presidential post in the next election?

Thirdly, on the question of economic relations between Taiwan and the mainland. We see extensive networks of functional relations between the mainland and Taiwan, by which I mean non-governmental contacts including trade, investment, tourism, cultural exchange, etc. It seems to me that these clearly describe the essence of evolving relations between Taiwan and the mainland. And I think that the PRC is just as preoccupied with how to manage the functional relations as the KMT is.

Earlier, Professor Nathan said the PRC will try everything they can to induce Taiwan's businessmen to become more involved in the mainland, and he asked how they are going to do that if no one is making money. I'm not sure about such an assessment. Some people are making money, others are not. A related question is: Who are investing there? As I see it, there are three groups of people interested in investment in China. The first are those who can't survive in Taiwan because they are in certain types of labor-intensive industries, are short of capital, and are manufacturers of low-end products. They have to go to the mainland to stay in business.

The second group are those who have a combination of political and economic interests. I'm talking about the few hundreds of Taiwan businessmen who followed delegations led by legislators to China in the early summer of 1990. In addition to hunting for photo-opportunities with the leaders of China, they also went to fish for investment projects. They hope that the PRC government will give them projects that will enable them to make money on the basis of their political connections. Unfortunately for most of them, they did not come home with many worthwhile projects.

The third category are those who should concern us the most: Taiwan's successful businessmen, including those from both big businesses and medium-size businesses, who are thinking of going to invest in China. From the scores of people I have spoken to, they were usually impressed with China during their first trip. During the second trip they began to complain about things in China. During the third trip, when they seriously investigated the details of investment, they came home and said, "Forget it, we'll wait for another time."

China is making every effort to see that more and more of the people of the third category go there. My impression is that they despise the second category. They don't really like the first category because most of the equipment they bring there is junk.

But they would like to attract the third category. So far they haven't succeeded, but they're going to offer something more attractive in the future. If we think in terms of five or six years, as China improves the investment environment and comes out with more attractive programs for Taiwan businessmen, do you see the possibility that Taiwan's business community can be transformed into a pressure group for China? And because most of those businessmen are Taiwanese, do you think this will eventually undermine indigenous Taiwanese identity?

Chu Yun-han
Can we foresee a day when the constitutional issues or the so-called "ground rules" issues are settled once and for all? I think from the viewpoint of the KMT, this is something next to an impossibility. Based on their past experience in dealing with the DPP with regard to constitutional reform issues, the KMT leaders believe that the DPP won't be ready any time soon to make a lasting commitment to a "grand compromise" over the constitutional issues. The DPP leaders might agree to a compromise reform package now, but it is highly likely they will shift their position three years later if later on the electoral prospects look different.

In short, the DPP might reasonably argue that as long as it is not given a fair electoral chance for competing with the KMT for the control of the government as well as for the dominance in orchestrating the process of democratic reforms and institutional rearrangement, there is no need for them to agree to any binding compromise. In responding to the KMT proposals of constitutional reform, the DPP currently cannot help but think in short-term strategic terms. I predict that the DPP will come to terms with the KMT over the constitutional reform issues only if the DPP experiences consecutive electoral defeats in the next two or three national elections, which by any account should be fairly competitive and open, and their hopes for a "new nation, new constitution" are dashed by lack of significant electoral support. Of course, it goes without saying that if the DPP defeats the KMT in the future elections, it will seek to overhaul the entire political system, including rewriting the constitution.

On the other hand, the KMT is not ready to deal with the more fundamental issues of ROC sovereignty and jurisdiction raised by the opposition. The KMT leaders figure that if in the next three to five years they manage to arrange for re-election of the three national representative bodies, implement the direct election of the provincial governor and the mayors of Taipei and Kaohsiung, and perhaps introduce an electoral college system for the selection of the president, then as far as the KMT is concerned they will have accomplished the task of constitutional reform.

Very likely, the election in 1992, and also the election in 1996, will be cast by both the KMT and the DPP as referenda on the two parties' divergent positions on constitutional issues. The DPP will also try to turn them into referenda on their stand on Taiwan independence. However, it is reasonable to predict that unless upset by an unexpected DPP gain, say a win of 45 percent of the legislative seats, the KMT will conclude that it is no longer vulnerable to attack from the DPP on democratic legitimacy and will refuse to negotiate further with the DPP.

Cheng Hsing-ti

In response to Professor Tien's question, I would like to say, first, I don't think the PRC's interference in KMT factional disputes is a real phenomenon. I think it is a little overplayed because there is no hard evidence to indicate that the PRC interfered in the so-called mainstream/non-mainstream dispute during the February 1990 political turmoil in Taiwan. Second, I think the rapprochement and interaction between the two sides of the Taiwan Straits will be accelerated in the coming decade. Third, I think the old guard of the CCP, such as Deng Xiaoping and Yang Shangkun, will fade away during the next decade. So I don't think the PRC will interfere in the 1996 presidential election.

Antonio Chiang

I have a different view from Professor Cheng's. I believe there was some kind of "China card" in the power struggle this past February–March. There was not necessarily a real negotiation with Beijing going on, but some kind of influence was very evident. In private discussions, people were very suspicious. In politics, trust is the most important thing. Trust is very intangible. You cannot prove that people are untrustworthy, yet you're suspicious of every move.

For instance, when Chiang Wei-kuo was in Washington, people were suspicious that he had something to do with Beijing. I don't believe it, but in private discussions, people like him, of his caliber, his background, said frankly that they distrust Lee Teng-hui, that they feel he is pro-independence. Some people have said very frankly to me that if Lee Teng-hui moves toward independence, they will go to the other side of the Taiwan Straits. In fact on the first of October, PRC's national day, some people went there to celebrate. They identify with China more than with Taiwan.

So there may not necessarily be a real dialogue going on, but the "China card" already is in Taiwan and in KMT politics. Its influence is obvious everywhere. That's the first point.

The second point has to do with business investment in China. There are so many businessmen going to Beijing to *pai-pai* (pay their respects), a kind of self-surrender. But I don't blame the businessmen because they have no motherland, they simply are pursuing profit. When Wang Yung-ching invests $7 billion on the mainland, that kind of investment transcends unification or independence. I don't think the independence people can criticize too much because on the one hand, Wang

Yung-ching has recovered the mainland; he and other Taiwanese businessmen are recovering the mainland for the Kuomintang. On the other hand, people like Wang create a kind of buffer zone in the coastal provinces. Just as people used to say that Hong Kong is occupying Guangdong and Taiwan is occupying Fujian, making this coastal region a buffer zone is good for our security, for peace in the Taiwan Straits.

Dr. Jason Hu paints a rosy picture. It seems that democracy will automatically take its own course. In 1996 we will be comfortably in democracy. I don't believe that kind of optimistic view. So far we see that all these elections, whether local or parliamentary, haven't counted. What really counts is the choice of the governor, the choice of the president. Among our national leaders, so far not one has been elected. In the year 1990, our per capita income exceeds $8000, and we have no right to elect our own national leaders. It is humiliating.

According to Dr. Hu's picture, we are electing the Legislative Yuan, we are appointing the new premier, we have intermediary organizations, we are going to elect a president six years from now. But we don't know if we really will be able to choose our premier or our president by that time. That's the most important knot that blocks our democracy. We have to cut this knot. This democratizing step by step is too slow. I don't think people have that kind of patience.

We are eliminating martial law. But the structure is still there, the laws are still there. The people who were high-ranking officers under martial law remain high-ranking officers now. So nothing has substantially changed. The structure is still there. Even though we have more elections, these elections do not change our political structure. We've had elections for forty years, but no real political leader came from elections. That kind of election cannot do much for our structure. I think that without the popular direct election of the premier or president, our democracy still has a long way to go.

Ying-mao Kau
What I'm going to say is not really a question. It's a general comment on the scenarios discussed this afternoon, particularly some of the more optimistic comments that the entire parliamentary membership will be changed by the end of next year, so you don't have to worry. I think in the long-term projection, I would agree the trend is there. The question, I think, for real politics and politicians is the day-to-day operation. How you can push democratization forward in a meaningful way, step by step. Every step counts. You cannot postpone the scenario until the year 2000, or 1997. The process itself is as important as the ultimate goal. As the joke says, in the long run we are all dead anyway. But in the short run, every step counts.

In this connection, I share the pain President Lee experienced last February and March. During the period of power struggle within the KMT, he was attacked as pro-Taiwan independence, as being too soft on the DPP, and so on. This criticism was orchestrated by *Liaowang* and *Renmin ribao*. That is really painful. That's the reason he has had to make such sacrifices by restructuring the cabinet leadership. I have great sympathy for him.

We are going to see greater democratization. But there are many concrete issues. For example, who is going to revise the constitution? The conservatives are still saying it has to be the existing National Assembly. Who are the majority? Nearly ninety percent of its members were elected forty-three years ago. Are we going to trust them to revise it? Some will say, "Oh, let them just play a little." According to the constitution and the Temporary Provisions, they can recall the president, they can change the constitution. That's the reason why this morning I suggested a broader-based constitutional reform commission. The issue of quotas, the ratio between the national constituency and the local constituency, the issue of how the president is going to be elected—there is no consensus yet on these issues and the struggle will continue.

If Taiwan is going to be fully democratized, party control over a number of important institutions must end. In the military, in the police, to some extent in education, and so on, it must end. How is that going to be done? It's very difficult. Mr. Chang Chün-hung talked about access to the television networks. We know TV greatly influences election outcomes. There are only three TV networks, and all are controlled by the government and the military. As long as this is the case, I do not think the elections can be fair or the results credible.

Earlier, we also talked about the issue of ethnic distribution of power. If you look at the military, people at the General level, or at police at the Bureau Chief level, the number of Taiwanese is still very small. A few percent. After forty years of democratic practice in Taiwan, that's an imbalanced situation that should be adjusted. I think these day-to-day operations are very important and more detailed attention should be paid to how to resolve them.

The Economic World of the 1990s and Taiwan's Place in It

Joseph Bosco
Taiwan's economy has grown very quickly, and the island has become recognized as one of the newly industrialized countries in the last ten years. Many people in Taiwan hope that this economic power can be translated into international recognition. So it's logical to begin today with the economics, and then to proceed in Panel Two to negotiating a place at the international table for Taiwan.

Chi Schive
About two years ago, a Japanese banker visited Taipei. After observing the situation in Taiwan, he began asking questions of his friends. He said, "Look, in the 1950s Japan began political democratization. It took ten years for Japan to accomplish this. Then in the 1960s Japan was short of labor, and the Japanese therefore had to learn to solve labor disputes. Again it took Japan ten years to solve the problem. Then came the 1970s, and Japan had to deal with the environmental protection issue. The 1980s now is the decade for Japan to move toward trade liberalization, removing trade barriers, and appreciating the Japanese yen sharply. In Taiwan," he concluded, "it seems the society must face these four issues at the same time. How are you going to do it?"

Definitely, Taiwan faces tremendous challenges on all fronts. Still worse, if that banker visited Taipei again, he would add another challenge. Our economy is in stagflation. In September 1990, the consumer price index in Taiwan went up 6.8 percent. That was the highest price rise in eight years. The industrial production index went down 2.5 percent from January to July 1990. That is a typical situation of stagflation.

In the early 1980s and the mid-1970s Taiwan had two earlier stagflations. There are some differences this time. The industrial production index over the last two years grew at a rate between 3 and 4 percent. In the past, if industrial production grew by only 3 or 4 percent, it was considered a recession. Why is it that this time no one talked about a recession until this year? Moreover, during the 1980s, the price level, including wholesale as well as consumer prices, went down. This didn't happen before. In other words the price level has been very stable in the 1980s.

The key to these differences is structural change. In 1986 the manufacturing sector accounted for 40 percent of Taiwan's GDP. I challenge you to find another country with such a high degree of dependence on the manufacturing sector. In 1989 the figure dropped to 35 percent. Over a rather short three or four years, you can see the relative importance of the manufacturing sector going down. Is that good or bad? According to Professor Simon Kuznets, a country goes through an industrialization stage first. Then, in a later stage, the economy relies on the service industry to provide the momentum of growth. Here you can see Taiwan's macroeconomic structure changing dramatically.

If we examine the industrial structure, we can also observe quite a few significant changes. Exports account for half of Taiwan's GDP. Over the past two or three years, if you divide export commodities into technology-intensive products versus less technology-intensive products, or divide exports into heavy and chemical industries versus light industries, you can see the significant changes in the proportions. In short, over the past three years, the industrial structure moved rapidly toward heavy industry, capital-intensive industry, and technology-intensive industry. That is another sign of structural change and the upgrading of industry.

One can also observe that over the past three years manufacturing-sector employment went down about five to six percent annually, for a total of approximately 16 percent. Again this is evidence of a significant structural change.

In the mid-1980s, Taiwan's economy was in macro-economic disequilibrium, both externally and internally. In 1986, the trade surplus accounted for 20 percent of Taiwan's total GDP—no other country except those oil-producing ones, especially no developing country, ever accumulated such a trade surplus. People talk about Japan's trade surplus, but in terms of GDP it amounts to no more than 4 percent. So 20 percent is not a normal situation.

For any country to have so large an external imbalance in trade means that the economy lacks investment. Such an economy is bound to have an excess of savings. To demonstrate the inadequacy of investment in Taiwan, let me cite another figure. Again in 1986, public investment, that is the investment carried out by the government, accounted for 3.6 percent of total GDP. In the 1970s in Japan, government spending on environmental protection alone accounted for 3 percent of GDP. Here you have to ask, how is it that the government on the one hand accumulated such a large foreign exchange reserve, and left it idle, while on the other hand the entire economy needs public investment so badly?

Could Taiwan continue to rely on manufacturing as the engine of growth? Could Taiwan rely on, or even promote increases in exports indefinitely? Could exports continue to be treated as the engine of growth? If the answers are no, then the economy has to be realigned and readjusted. And such a transition is taking place.

What are the impacts, and what results can be expected when the economy is in the process of adjustment? Number one, as you can observe, the New Taiwan Dollar appreciated somewhere around 50 percent. The strength of the local currency creates an incentive and a pressure is created for outward investment. Over the past three years, the estimated outward investment was somewhere around $20 billion. Over the past four years, the export of machinery increased more than 30 percent and is now the second largest export item in Taiwan, second only to electronics. This is the impact of outward investment. From this you can see the role Taiwan can play on the international economic scene, especially in Southeast Asia but also in mainland China.

In order to adjust the imbalance, one thing we would expect is more attention to domestic demand. You can see this in the growth of the service industry and the financial sector. I will leave the details to the next speaker, but it is clear that the service industry will grow and will overtake the manufacturing sector. It is safe also to predict that high-tech industries will become more important.

What will happen during the next decade? What are the prospects for Taiwan's development in the long run? As an economist I think prediction is much easier than it is for a political scientist. We know that for an economy to grow, you need four things. In the short run, the efficiency of resource allocation plays the dominant role. In practical terms what does this mean? It means you have to remove protection and subsidies, raise management efficiency through privatization, and assure adequate investment.

Number two, technological progress is also a very important factor. Third, education, training, and manpower policy are important. Fourth, let me cite one sentence from Adam Smith. He says that an economy can grow to the full complement of its riches as permitted by its law and its institutions, and there it rests. What we see in Taiwan today is that the institutions, the laws, may not cope with the current situation. This implies that for Taiwan's economy to grow we need reform of our institutions.

Paul S.P. Hsu

My talk grows out of the point just raised by Professor Schive. I want to point to three or four of the areas in which government policy, especially laws and regulations, lag behind industry.

First is the service industry. The indicator of whether the government is providing encouragement to a particular sector of industry is, number one, whether there are tax incentives, and number two, whether they allow foreign investors to get involved in that business. Since Taiwan didn't have much of a service industry in the modern sense, it's obvious that foreign investments are required to help the initial growth of those industries.

Let's look at advertising, department stores, and the fast food industry. There are no tax incentives for these service industries. But then the service industry didn't ask for tax incentives, so that's not a factor in that particular sector. But how about allowing foreign investment? Allowing foreign investment means the government gives the foreign investor repatriation privileges on earnings and capital in case the foreign investor liquidates the investment or sells shares. Some time ago the foreign advertising industry began cooperative programs with the local advertising industry. But there was a big problem. The foreign advertising company could not take an equity position and whatever they earned they could not repatriate. The same was the case in the department store and fast food industries. It was about five years after these industries began to move into Taiwan or began to show an interest in doing so that the government finally lifted these restrictions. Meanwhile, there are many ways to skin a cat. If foreign investment is not allowed, the foreign investor can waive the repatriation privilege and keep the money as blocked funds in Taiwan. Many did so. In the fast food industry they charged their "profit" through transfer pricing on raw materials.

An even more important example concerns capital markets and financial services. The government had a program back in 1983 to encourage venture capital and mutual funds, but after that there was a long period of not making any further moves.

That was probably one of the primary reasons for the offshoot of underground investment houses because the door was not opened sufficiently to allow a full range of capital market activities and to regulate it.

Finance and credit companies are absolutely important to industries. When the manufacturer accepts payment by installments, they have to put the accounts receivable on their books. But if they are allowed to run a separate company to do the financing of their product, they can remove the accounts receivable from their books. This creates a much more solid financial condition for the manufacturer and allows them to borrow more funds to expand. So far, the government has not allowed or regulated separate finance and credit companies. In the U.S., General Motors has it, Ford has it, General Electric has it.

In the absence of government licensing, people have said that trading companies can play this role. Since a trading company can sell, it can also do installment sales. Unofficially, through the trading company mechanism, credit companies are in operation in Taiwan, yet we are still waiting for the formal laws and regulations allowing them.

The same is true in investment activities. Only a few days ago the Legislative Yuan approved a revision of the company law. One of the most important changes was to remove the restriction that prevents a company from investing in other companies in an aggregate amount exceeding 40 percent of its own paid-in capital. That makes it virtually impossible for a Taiwan-based company to do mergers and acquisitions abroad. Have Taiwan companies been doing mergers and acquisitions abroad? Of course, they've been doing them for years. Continental Engineering bought American Bridge, which built the Empire State Building in the thirties and the Sears Tower in the sixties. How did they do it? They raised funds outside Taiwan, in order not to violate the law against exceeding 40 percent of their own paid-in capital.

These examples show that the private sector in Taiwan is ahead of government laws, regulations, and policy.

I fully agree with Professor Chi Schive that the future economic prospects for Taiwan very much depend on the allocation of resources. Financial resources, in my opinion, will continue to grow. The question is how to establish a more efficient capital and financial market. That requires very prudent, far-sighted government policy, laws, and regulations.

Take the example of the huge amount of accumulated pension funds in Taiwan. The government's intention was good: the pension funds belong to labor, let's not play around with that. And therefore, let's give it to only one totally government-owned financial institution, called The Central Trust, to manage. Managing large pension funds requires expertise if you want to have higher yield. But the fact is, they want to be very conservative, so as to protect the funds. Therefore the yield is maybe 4 percent or 5 percent, certainly very low. Those funds, under current laws and regulations, cannot be made available for a professional manager to manage, and that's a waste of financial resources. The question of how to prudently utilize Taiwan's financial resources, whether in the form of extra savings or in the form of government foreign exchange reserves, deserves our closest attention.

Secondly, manpower resources. This depends on improving the educational system and close cooperation between Taiwan's educational system and foreign educational institutions. That's an area in which nature will also take its course, based on the anxiety of Chinese families to enhance their children's education. But manpower resources also includes skilled workers, technicians, and mid-management personnel.

We also have to learn how to package technology and know-how in order to create licensing packages, or technical cooperation, or technical assistance packages—in other words, turn them into valuable commodities. One more resource I want to mention is the strong entrepreneurial spirit that we have witnessed over the decades.

I now want to outline a few other thoughts I have in regard to Taiwan's role in the world economy of the 1990s. One point concerns Taiwan's possible role in what has been called "the Chinese-based economy," not bound to any particular territorial boundary, any particular political or social system. I want to use the term *Hua-jen*, instead of *Chung-kuo*, to appease our colleagues from countries like Singapore.

One example is Dr. An Wang, the founder of Wang Laboratories. He established a totally American-oriented company. But when he started thinking about raising a venture capital fund to invest under a diversified scheme, he went to Taiwan and raised a $50 million dollar fund. This shows one of the roles Taiwan can play in the Chinese-based economy. That Chinese-based economy would naturally cover the PRC, Singapore, Hong Kong, etc.

Taiwan can play a role in the East Asian regional economy—that would cover Indonesia, the Philippines, Thailand, and Malaysia—and in the world economy. Yesterday I cited the example of a group of Taiwan businessmen who formed a consortium, went to Ireland, and established an industrial park. That is a good example of close cooperation between the private sector and the government sector, representing a new phenomenon. The government provided a $20 million soft loan at a low interest rate. That's quite a good example of the role Taiwan can play in the world economy. Another ten or twenty industrial parks in different parts of the world can be established in the years to come, if so desired.

Taiwan is a small place if you look at the world map, and Taiwan's resources are not unlimited. But certainly, there are many roles Taiwan can play in the Chinese-based, regional, and world economies.

What is the next practical step? I suggest the private and public sectors in Taiwan should aggressively internationalize Taiwan's businesses and economy first. And I believe we should not get too closely tied to the PRC. There are too many political, social, and other issues to deal with. So I envision an aggressive internationalization effort in which Taiwan should go out and establish its place in the Chinese-based economy, the East Asian regional economy, and the world economy.

Let's work on this for five years, and then come back and sit down with PRC and say, "Look, we are a part of the world economy. We are not just representing interests in Taiwan alone." Similarly, instead of waiting for 1997 to fall on their heads, the Hong Kong Chinese should merge Hong Kong's economy into the world economy as well. Then they could take a more aggressive stand with the PRC leaders, not in the form of pointing fingers or saying you did this wrong, you did that wrong, but by saying this is the way a world economy works. If you want this result, this is what is required. It takes a special kind of initiative to do this, but I feel the Hong Kong Chinese have the capability to do it.

And not just in Hong Kong. Chinese in other Chinese-based economies can do the same. I think somebody should begin an effort to constructively influence the Chinese leaders in their thinking toward the future.

A final remark from a Chinese economic history viewpoint. Perhaps Professor Chi Schive, as a trained economist, can confirm this. In Chinese economic history, economic development always has been inward. We on Taiwan, and Chinese in other Chinese-based economies, represent a totally new element in Chinese economic history. Here is a group of Chinese who are trained, experienced, and accomplished in an outward-looking type of economy. To use old terminology, an ocean-going economy instead of inland economy; and it will change the Chinese economic history of the future.

N.T. Wang

I feel that my predecessors were really on safe ground. Professor Chi Schive talked of what happened three years ago, and Mr. Hsu spoke about what the government should do. As a less prudent man, I will not play it safe but will try to deal directly with my assigned topic. First I will address the question, what will the economic world of the 1990s be like? Second, what will Taiwan's place in this world be? I will make five points relevant to each question. Since the megatrends are interrelated, understanding the economic world is essential to understanding Taiwan's place in it.

The first point is that there will be major changes in the fortunes of different nations in the world. The relative decline of U.S. power is already fairly evident. The rising power of Japan, Western Europe, and the Pacific economies is likely to continue into the 1990s. The trend may not accelerate, but changes will cumulate in magnitude in the coming decade as mechanisms to reverse the fortunes of the laggards become less effective.

The second point is that as a result of the shifting fortunes of nations all sorts of new power centers will emerge. Gone are the days of Pax Britannica. Gone also are all the days of Pax Americana or of two superpowers. This is best illustrated by the necessity for one superpower to beg for food. The point is also dramatically brought home by the Gulf crisis engineered by a small power. Consequently, the world structure is characterized by multiple powers, old and new, big and small, rather than by a single or dual hegemony. It is reminiscent of the Warring States period in Chinese history. The leaderlessness of world affairs is likely to become more serious when the United States belatedly realizes the limits of its power and behaves accordingly. A sense of powerlessness will become pervasive.

The third point is a natural outcome of the second. Without a clear, single (or dual) leader there will be a decline in world order. As the old world order erodes, the clamor for a new world order will become more vocal. Such calls, however, do not have enough muscle to replace the old order but merely help to further erode its credibility. Efforts at compromise are difficult on account of differences in values as well as interests. There will be increasing uncertainty in the development of world events. No one is in, or capable of, control.

The fourth point is a manifestation of the third. Again taking a leaf from the history of the Warring States period, there will be a tendency to form all sorts of groups or alliances. This will be most evident in the field of world trade. As the rules of the game enshrined in multilateralism are eroded by increasing exceptions, such as voluntary restraints, quotas, discriminatory treatments, multifiber arrangements, and unilateral threats, bilateralism and blocism flourish. Countries with strong bargaining power tend to resort to bilateral arrangements in order to exact gains from the relatively weak and grant special favors to client countries and territories. This in turn gives incentives for others to form blocs to raise their bargaining power. Thus, the European Community openly aims at containing the power of the United States. Conversely, the evolving American bloc, comprising first the United States and Canada, and extending possibly to Mexico and other Latin American countries, is a response to the European development.

The fifth point is complimentary to the fourth. For the erosion of multilateralism does not result in complete anarchy or autarky. The increase in international interdependence is irreversible. The world has shrunk with revolutions in transportation and communications, and in the ease of cross-border movements of capital, skilled labor, management, and technology. No country, however rich in population or space, can ignore its relationship with the rest of the world. To do so on the ground of old-fashioned self-reliance or avoidance of *dependencia* would be suicidal. Moreover, the world market will become increasingly competitive simply because there will be more and more players as the monopoly of economic power by a few nations breaks down. Under such circumstances the traditional measure of monopolistic power, the industry concentration ratio (the share of production accounted for by three or four of the largest firms in an industry), misses the point when imports become readily available, as witnessed in the automobile industry in the United States. But although the competition will be fiercer, it will by no means be atomistic as defined by the textbooks. The real world will become more complicated.

If we accept the picture of the world of the 1990s that I have just painted, Taiwan's place in it will have the following five characteristics.

First is the end of the Golden Age of the last four decades. I do not, of course, imply that the international environment was ideal in this period. Formally, a state of war persisted with mainland China. Nonetheless, what is significant is that until recently the rest of the world had by and large treated Taiwan with benign neglect. Even if the mode of competition pursued by Taiwan's international traders did not meet the then accepted international rules of the game, the trade volume and its impact on others were insufficiently alarming to warrant the trouble of serious scrutiny or retaliation. Where such scrutiny arose, fairly or unfairly, as in quantitative restrictions, anti-dumping or countervailing duties, the effect on Taiwan was manageable through flexible adjustments. In the 1990s Taiwan's very success has placed it in a different league.

On the domestic front as well, the benign authoritarian rule of the past four decades awarded much political challenge or factional tugs of war. Government policy and administration had a fairly free hand, largely unimpeded by conflicting demands. However, with the gradual introduction of democratic institutions and procedures, most economic issues will become politicized.

Second, a corollary of the first point, the Taiwan miracle has signaled graduation from the ranks of developing economies.

Thus, not only is Taiwan ineligible for international aid but it is increasingly expected to participate as a donor. The removal of Taiwan from the list of exporters that enjoy the Generalized System of Preferences is another clear shift. Taiwan will increasingly be expected to play by the rules that other developed countries are supposed to follow, in fields such as subsidies, intellectual property, and finance. "Small is beautiful" is no longer applicable to Taiwan. Nor does the notion that Taiwan has already achieved takeoff in its development ensure its future smooth sailing.

Third, while Taiwan's phenomenal economic successes have been accomplished in spite of persistent reverses in active participation in the world community, its second-class international status will impede its further efforts at internationalization. At the beginning of the 1990s Taiwan had lost its seat in most international economic organizations. The pursuit of flexible diplomacy, evidenced by Taiwan's remaining in the Asian Development Bank despite its loss of the China seat, applying for entry to the General Agreement on Tariffs and Trade as a customs area, and negotiating semiofficial representations and tax and investment arrangements with countries without diplomatic ties, may achieve limited goals. Yet it is unlikely to alter the basic situation in which the major powers are not derecognizing the mainland regime. The recent reestablishment of diplomatic relations with a few small countries at the cost of huge donations appears to be of dubious practical value.

Fourth, there is an increasing sense of isolation internationally. This is most evident in trade relations. If multilateralism suffers from further erosion following the lack of progress in GATT negotiations, and the European Community turns into a fortress Europe after 1992, and America forms its own bloc, who are Taiwan's potential partners? Taiwan does not enjoy the special favored status of former colonies of members of the European twelve, nor does it fall within the traditional geographic scope of the Monroe Doctrine. As far as an Asian bloc is concerned, both its appropriate membership and its functions are yet to be formulated and negotiated. How much voice will Taiwan have in this process?

Fifth, in view of all the above, the emerging economic relationship with the mainland will play a key role in determining Taiwan's place in the world. To be sure, barring unforeseen political developments, progress in reunification with the mainland is likely to be slow. At the same time, the application of the principle of flexible diplomacy to relations with the mainland should permit a growing economic relationship even without a political breakthrough. The path of this relationship has already been broken by almost two million Taiwanese visitors to the mainland since 1987. Taiwanese trade and investment in the mainland has already transformed a number of coastal areas, such as Xiamen, into boom towns, and the tendency is to spread into other areas not only in Fujian, where cultural affinity with Taiwan is most evident, but also in Guangdong, Shanghai, and other open areas.

From the point of view of Taiwan, the relocation of labor-intensive industries, such as shoes, umbrellas, and textiles, to the mainland where labor costs are far lower, even after allowance for lower productivity, is a matter of survival. However, the application of comparative advantage by no means stops here. The mainland possesses many natural resources, such as petroleum and minerals; key industries, such as machinery and chemicals; as well as skilled labor, such as medical and computer specialists. In the pursuit of internationalization and liberalization Taiwan can hardly ignore the mainland factor. If Taiwan's industries are to remain competitive, the mainland connection must be compared with other alternatives, such as the ASEAN countries. The question remains as to whether the economic calculus will be overshadowed by political objections.

In a separate paper, I have argued that the current political arguments, such as security and *dependencia*, against expanding economic relations with the mainland are overblown. At the same time, granted that it takes two to tango and given the disparity in size and the historical enmity between Taiwan and the mainland, a more imaginative and accommodating initiative is to be expected from the mainland to permit Taiwan to gain a rightful place in the world. Whether such an initiative will be forthcoming within the decade of the 1990s, I do not have the crystal ball to tell, but I will be disappointed with the Chinese if they do not have the same courage and vision as the East and West Germans in rejoining their hands to shape their future in this increasingly competitive world.

—Floor Discussion—

Dennis Engbarth (Senior Editor, *Business International*)
I'd like to ask Professor Chi Schive how long he expects the current stage of stagflation to last. And also, please discuss the key factors that would help either to assist or to impede the recovery of the Taiwan economy.

Chi Schive
The key factor to watch is how fast the government can speed up investment. If the government can solve industry's problems, for example by acquiring land, bringing in immigrant labor, and settling environmental protection disputes, then I think the government can really put money to work. So far as I know, the current figure for public investment as a percentage of total GDP is going up, but still stays around 5 percent. Compared to the previous peak, that is still low.

The other point relates to public enterprises or government companies. Here we are talking about investment by the Chinese Petroleum Company and the Taiwan Power Company. If construction starts on the fourth nuclear power plant, then you are talking about billions in investment. So if that happens, then obviously effective demand would be created very fast. If this does not happen, and if the world recession is quite bad, then I will make a brave guess and say that the Taiwan dollar will be devalued. Taiwan's exports are declining because on the one hand we have domestic inflation, while on the other hand appreciation of the NT dollar has reached 50 percent. Under these conditions, how can Taiwan maintain the growth rate of exports equivalent to that of the GNP? The growth rate of exports now is zero.

How long the recession will last, I don't know. It really depends on whether or not domestic demand can be increased rapidly. If that fails, then, because exports are still around 50 percent of Taiwan's GDP, you cannot really let exports go down sharply, for example by 10 percent. Instead of allowing that to happen, I think the government would just go for NT dollar depreciation.

Paul Chu (Attorney, Cathay International)
I have two questions. Apparently, there are two points that are important for Taiwan's economic development. One is structural change. And the second is internationalization of the economy. The first question is addressed to Professor Chi Schive about structural change.

If structural change is mismanaged, the economy could move backward, just like in the Philippines. In view of the 80 percent drop in the capital market, what is Professor Chi Schive's view on resource allocation? What can the government do, in terms of policy, to promote a more efficient market in allocating financial resources?

The second question is addressed to Professor Wang about the internationalization of Taiwan's economy. Professor Wang stressed the strategic importance of an alliance with mainland

China. But there is a lot of concern in Taiwan that there might be a conspiracy on mainland China's part to attract Taiwan's capital and then turn around and shut the door, with terrible consequences for the Taiwan economy. What do you think? Is there such a conspiracy on mainland China's part?

Chi Schive
Everyone knows that the stock market in Taiwan fell about 80 percent. People are talking about damage to Taiwan's economy. But first you have to ask why the stock market went up so fast. In 1986 the growth rate of money supply was 48 percent. The next year it was 37 percent, and the year after that 24 percent. For any economy, if you observe such growth in the money supply, what do you expect? You expect inflation. But in Taiwan there was no inflation. At the same time, this also was the period when Taiwan really got into trade liberalization by sharp appreciation of the NT dollar, by cutting the nominal tariff rate from around 30 percent to below 10 percent, and by removing most import controls except on a very few items, such as cars. Import prices were stable. And, thank God, oil prices were going down.

A strange situation was created. There was money everywhere, yet prices were stable. That means the interest rate was going down. If interest rates are going down, people start thinking that if they put their money into a savings account and earn 3 percent and 4 percent interest, this is nothing. So people begin going into the stock market, and you can see all the money flooding in. The result is the rise of stock prices, which makes you happy, makes me happy, and makes everyone feel wealthy. Last year, imported cars accounted for around 40 percent of the total cars purchased. Who are the buyers of the imported cars? They are people spending some of the money they made in the stock market.

If the price of the stock market is far from real value, in other words if the price of the stock cannot be supported by the economic strengths of the economy, then it will go down. That is why right now in Taiwan the businesses are crying for the government's help. And I think that is the price we have to pay. The stock market bubble is expected to burst, and it will eventually. However, when things are going back to normal and becoming stable, the new situation will facilitate the economy's going through the transition period mentioned at the beginning, i.e., to put more resources back into the domestic economy quickly and properly.

N.T. Wang

It's very nice of Paul to ask me this question because it gives me a chance to explain what I meant by strategic alliances. I have very much in mind, for example, the strategic alliance between General Motors and Toyota. You do realize that Toyota is a very tough competitor, but at the same time you look around the world and the question is whether you have an alliance with Toyota or not. Of course, you don't want to be completely dependent on Toyota, otherwise you will lose your shirt in the end. So what I mean by a strategic alliance is that Taiwan wants to look at the whole world in terms of the best location of resources, and where you should choose your partners. And I feel that in many cases it is going to be in China, as Hong Kong has discovered, and not only for the shoe industry, toy industry, garment industry, and textile industry. Hong Kong entrepreneurs have learned that if you locate in Hong Kong, you cannot compete in the world anymore, so you have to locate certain facilities in the mainland. But that doesn't mean that you put all your resources on the mainland. You are still in control. You are deciding, just as General Motors decides, or IBM, and so on, where you want to locate certain facilities. If the government says that you can't go to the mainland, then you choose second best, third best places, and if your competitive advantage is lessened, that would be bad for the upgrading of the Taiwan economy.

I realize that a lot of people in Taiwan still are very much afraid of communism and anything to do with communism. The top people on the mainland would really like to see unification with Taiwan. That has been their dream for the last fifty, maybe sixty years. They would like to achieve it in their lifetime. But if they lure the Taiwanese into the mainland, and then all of a sudden say, "Now you are our hostage and we will take over," that would be quite stupid because the effect would put all hopes of reunification out of the question.

In Fujian or Guangdong, or similar places in China, you find that the cadres and even the provincial and municipal heads see their fortunes very much linked with foreign investment. That's how these territories are developing. So there is an overriding interest to see that these investments continue to work and to prosper.

Finally, I go back to my point that Taiwan should be playing the multinational role. In other words, if the mainland should take the enterprises over, they would have the physical plant but they wouldn't be able to make it work. For example, the shoe factories are over there. But the entrepreneurs are still calling the shots as to what kind of shoes to be produced, where they are to be marketed, and through what networks all over the world. If you leave everything to the mainland Chinese, they would be totally lost and the factories would just not be worth anything to take over.

Negotiating a Place at the Table: Taiwan's Role in the International Community of the 1990s

Harvey J. Feldman
It's obvious that there's a disconnection between Taiwan's considerable economic weight and its minuscule political weight. Taiwan is recognized diplomatically by a only handful of second- and third-ranked countries and is spending, as Professor N.T. Wang pointed out, perhaps too much of its resources courting the recognition of ministates. Is this a wise pattern for the conduct of international relations in the 1990s? What will flexible diplomacy mean? How should it operate? Can Taiwan come back into the multilateral world? It has applied to GATT. Could it even get into organizations like the World Health Organization, which does not restrict membership to nation states? How can it translate economic muscle into viable political relationships?

Ying-mao Kau
The title of this panel, "Negotiating a Place at the Table," reminds me of an editorial in the *Houston Chronicle* last year. The editorial said that the community of nations, which doesn't accept Taiwan, has begun to grumble that Taiwan is so rich, it could be of help. Among the latest is U.S. Treasury Secretary Nicholas Brady, who has suggested that Taiwan is capable of helping solve the Third World debt problem. The editorial concluded by saying that it may be the way the world works, but there is something wrong with saying that you can help to pay for the meals, but you cannot have a seat at the table.

Before we discuss how Taiwan can negotiate a place in the world community, I think it's worth reviewing what kind of situation Taiwan seems to be in in terms of its international involvement. The downturn in Taiwan's diplomatic fortunes started in 1971 when the Republic of China was expelled from the UN and the seat was taken over by the PRC. At one point diplomatic recognition of Taiwan was down to 21 countries. Recently, it increased to 28, but now it is probably down to 26. In terms of Taiwan's participation in International Governmental Organizations (IGOs), the Foreign Ministry recently counted 10. However, aside from the Asian Development Bank and Interpol, you probably would not recognize the names of those organizations, which suggests the rest are insignificant. Even in Interpol, because of the problem of names and status, Taiwan has not really participated in the past several years.

In terms of Taiwan's diplomatic recognition, you can say there are 26 who recognize it. But these 26 countries are rather small. Over half have populations of less than 300,000. More than half of them do not have even a million dollars in two-way trade with Taiwan. The more important countries were Saudi Arabia, which was lost recently, and South Korea, where relations apparently are in serious trouble. Another important country is South Africa, but of course this is a country with a lot of problems of its own.

Probably 137 countries recognize the PRC as the sole legal government of China. At present, 37 or 38 major IGOs take the PRC as the representative of China. Under those circumstances, Taiwan has had to concentrate on development of the so-called substantive relations. This means that Taiwan develops cultural, economic, technical, and trade relations with various countries without official connections. Taiwan has significant trade and economic ties with 120 countries out of the 175 countries in the world. Taiwan has established some sort of semi-official offices in 41 countries, and 20 or so countries have also established offices in Taiwan.

The substantive area of interactions is of course very important for Taiwan's economic and technological survival. But substantive relations are no substitute for official relations. This is particularly true in terms of access to high-level government offices in various countries, decent consular services for the nationals of the Republic of China, negotiating trade and tariff issues, and so on. But above all, it affects Taiwan's defense capabilities. Taiwan has got to have access to military weapons systems, access to the so-called dual use technology which can be used for both military as well as civilian purposes. Luckily, the Taiwan Relations Act enabled Taiwan to have continued access to U.S. defensive weapons, which is absolutely important. Without this access, I think that Taiwan would have been long gone as an independent entity after 1979.

Lack of international status is beginning to have a serious impact on internal politics, as was pointed out in previous sessions. Taiwan is emerging as an important economic power in terms of its GNP, GNP per capita, trade, foreign currency reserves, and so on. When the citizens of the country perceive the country as a major economic power, contributing importantly to the world arena, but not being treated fairly, they are going to demand that their government do something about it.

In the 1950s and 1960s Taiwanese didn't have much opportunity to travel abroad, and foreign policy was seen as an exclusive preserve of the foreign policy elite. But recent statistics suggest that 70 percent of the adult population in Taiwan now travel abroad, and that is quite significant. They have direct contact with foreign countries, and that means they have to take the passport of the Republic of China, and apply for visas to various countries. If you just focus on the visa business, roughly forty countries have offices in Taiwan to which visa applications can be filed. For others, you may have to go through some sort of unofficial channel, private corporations, and so on, to apply for a visa. This creates a lot of frustration for people because time is wasted. Sometimes you are required to have twelve pictures, and with guarantors, etc. Therefore people begin to question the ability of the government to protect the national interest and the ability of the country to survive in the international arena.

The issue of international identity has begun to have a significant internal impact. For some, the sentiment for independence is mainly in order to break out of international isolation and gain the kind of respect and dignity that the people on Taiwan deserve.

Government policy seems to be rather rigid in terms of raising the status of Taiwan in the international community. We are familiar with the doctrine of *Han tsei pu liang-li*, the government and the bandits cannot coexist, and the ROC's continued claim to be the sole legal government of all China. In the 1950s and 1960s emphasis on this principle benefitted Taiwan's diplomatic status because more countries recognized Taiwan, the Republic of China, than recognized the PRC. Also, Taiwan occupied a seat in the UN, including a seat at the Security Council. So by making this a zero-sum game, Taiwan was able, with the help of the United States, to exclude the PRC from the international arena. After 1971, the picture changed. At that point continuing the zero-sum game meant that Taiwan was going to suffer. In fact, it became a self-imposed restriction on Taiwan's ability to develop diplomatic relationships. At one point it was so rigid that when countries that recognized the PRC began to talk about the possibility of simultaneous recognition of the Republic of China, as I understand it, the Foreign Ministry instructed its diplomats to demand that those countries break relations with the PRC first before they could be recognized by the ROC.

The policy began to change after Lee Teng-hui took over leadership in January 1988. At the Thirteenth Party Congress of the KMT, Lee Teng-hui argued that Taiwan should not be satisfied with relations at the substantive level, and that efforts should be made to break out of isolation. The major conceptual breakthrough came in March 1989 when he visited Singapore at the invitation of Lee Kuan-yew. Even though there were no diplomatic relations, the president of the Republic of China went anyway, and at his press conference after his return he enunciated a number of important principles. He was willing to modify the *Han tsei pu liang-li*, or the Republic of China is the sole legal government, attitude. The zero-sum game doctrine would be modified. He also indicated his willingness for peaceful coexistence with the PRC, and, if necessary, dual recognition. His argument was that dual recognition is not done at the initiative of Taiwan, but it is the business of recognizing countries to decide. He also indicated that he would be willing to mobilize Taiwan's newly gained economic resources to support diplomatic breakthroughs.

From these concepts emerged what we now know as pragmatic or flexible diplomacy. Since 1989 there have been a series of developments trying to put this new concept into practice. Shirley Kuo was sent to Beijing, the "bandit" capital, to participate in the ADB (Asian Development Bank) annual meeting. A number of countries such as Grenada, Liberia, Belize, Lesotho, and so on, which had recognized the PRC as the sole legal government of China, opened up diplomatic ties with Taiwan. The OECDF (Overseas Economic Cooperation and Development Fund) was established with $1.2 billion in capital to support Third World development, essentially to mobilize economic resources to support diplomatic efforts. A relief fund for Third World countries, the Humanitarian Relief Fund, was also established. In the United States and other developed countries, the Chiang Ching-kuo Foundation was established to deal with cultural and academic exchanges and can also be considered part of Taiwan's more active participation in the world arena.

The concept of pragmatic diplomacy also brought Lee Teng-hui into serious trouble. In the political crisis in the spring of 1990, much criticism by conservatives was related to Lee's pragmatic diplomacy. He was accused of supporting or engineering a two China or one China–one Taiwan policy, and even of supporting Taiwan independence. These charges by the conservatives were further orchestrated by the PRC to criticize Lee Teng-hui and as the rationalization for gestures, including a military buildup, to oppose Lee's diplomatic initiatives.

This really is a tragedy for Taiwan's diplomatic efforts. If you cannot get support internally to try to break out of international isolation, and, in addition, the PRC gets involved in attacking the policy, then practicing pragmatic policy becomes even more difficult. There is a saying in Taiwan that diplomacy is an extension of internal politics, and I think it's quite true. If internal politics features a conservative backlash, Lee Teng-hui is going to have greater difficulty in implementing his policy. Nevertheless, he is a person of vision, and he can be very stubborn. I think he is convinced that pragmatic diplomacy, under the principle of one China, is the right way to go. My personal feeling is that he will continue to push, and I think that he is going to have the support of the people of Taiwan.

Tsai Shih-yuan

I am delighted to have this opportunity to talk to so many distinguished people who are concerned about the future of the TPKM. Just in case anyone still does not know what the TPKM is, well, the TPKM is the name used by the Taiwan government early in 1990 to apply for membership in GATT, the General Agreement on Tariffs and Trade. This unusual alphabet soup stands for Taiwan, Penghu, Kinmen (Chinmen), and Matsu. So I am a National Assemblyman from the TPKM.

The fact that the Taiwan government is proposing a designation other than the Republic of China is of some importance. For a long time now, in spite of the opposition's call for more flexibility, the Taiwan government has insisted on using the name Republic of China, with the connotation that it is the sole, legitimate government of China, which in their view includes Taiwan. (The names "Taipei, China" as used in the Asian Development Bank and "Chinese Taipei" in the International Olympic Committee were imposed on them and accepted under protest.)

It might be stretching the logic too far to infer from the government's proposing a new name that there is a change in the basic attitude of the Taiwan government. But surely when such a change comes from a government that has legendarily claimed sovereignty over China after it has been expelled from China for more than forty years, there must be compelling reasons. I would like to suggest that, although compelling reasons might be found in the areas of economic benefit and international politics, the major reason in the final analysis lies in domestic political competition.

My assertion is that there is a need for political leaders in Taiwan to show their determination to gain membership for Taiwan in major international organizations, or they will risk losing popular support to their political competitors.

There is a strong consensus on Taiwan that we should enter major international organizations. This is not yet a hot political issue, but it has the potential to be one in the 1990s. The economic reasons behind this consensus are easy to understand. Taiwan, whose international trade totaled $118 billion in 1989 and which is the twelfth largest trading nation in the world, simply cannot afford to be isolated internationally from the established venues of international decision making. With its $70 billion of foreign reserves and an increasingly protectionistic international environment, Taiwan needs to have access to international political discourse and dispute-arbitration mechanisms.

Taiwan also stands to gain by entering international organizations such as GATT, whose members normally accord one another mutual most-favored-nation status.

The timing of popular demand to enter international

organizations is related to recent developments in international politics. The vast change in Eastern Europe and the Soviet Union under Gorbachev has reduced the strategic importance of the People's Republic of China in the eyes of the United States and Western Europe. The Tiananmen massacre on June 4, 1989, outraged the world. This seems to be a good time to gain international support for Taiwan to enter international organizations.

The consensus for entering international organizations seems to rest more on a psychological need for security against the threats of the PRC than on grounds of international political development or economics. It can be argued that Taiwan has been so successful in economic development in the past twenty years of international isolation that there is no reason it cannot continue to do so through unofficial relations to the world. Besides, membership in the major organizations might mean that Taiwan will have to make the painful decision to give up its "Buy American" policy and extend most-favored-nation status to Japan and even to the PRC. The mid- and short-term economic benefits do not seem sufficient to generate such a high level of consensus to enter international organizations.

The importance of membership in the major international organizations for Taiwanese domestic politics can be intuitively felt through some unlikely, hypothetical questions. Let us assume for argument's sake that it is certain that Taiwan can enter the United Nations under the designation of the "Republic of China on Taiwan," and can do so only under this designation. The KMT would have no difficulty accepting this name, but the DPP might. What would happen to the DPP if it stated, "No, we do not agree to this and would rather not enter the UN than accept such a ridiculous name"? My guess is that popular support of the DPP would erode overnight.

Now let us turn the hypothetical question around and assume that it is absolutely certain that Taiwan can enter the UN, but only under the designation "Taiwan." The DPP would have no difficulty with it. But what about the KMT? What would happen to the KMT if it still insisted, "No, we are not Taiwan"? Would people still support the KMT and allow it to remain in a decision-making capacity? I doubt it.

These hypothetical questions are meant to show the potential strength of the popular demand for Taiwan to enter international organizations. And it also shows that people on Taiwan are more flexible than their political leaders on the problem of designation, which seems to be one of the major obstacles in entering some international economic organizations.

As Taiwan democratizes, popular support on important issues will be critical to the success or failure of political parties. "Entering international organizations" ranks high among these important issues because it fulfills the psychological need for security. Political leaders will need to take a position on this issue that is consistent with public demand. Therefore, I predict that in 1990s there will be aggressive attempts to enter international organizations and gain diplomatic recognition, and there will be flexibility on designations, including the names "Taiwan" or "Republic of Taiwan" or whatever. This will be done regardless of Taiwanese political leaders' positions on the future relationship between Taiwan and China or their positions on the international status of Taiwan. This will be true despite the KMT's present unwillingness to try everything and anything to gain diplomatic recognition. Flexibility about names seems limited only by a clear desire to avoid any implication that Taiwan is a local government under the PRC, or that PRC jurisdiction extends to Taiwan.

Taiwan has moved along the path of democratization by bypassing the question of independence/unification. The same strategy could be followed vis-à-vis international organizations by adopting a name that is capable of various explanations, leaving enough room for the PRC to say whatever it wants to say, while the KMT can say that its pragmatic diplomacy is aimed at eventual reunification, and the DPP can say that it proves the sovereignty of Taiwanese people over Taiwan.

The PRC should not underestimate the substantive and psychological importance to the people of Taiwan of entering international organizations. By entering organizations such as GATT, OECD, PECC, the World Bank, IMF, and the UN, Taiwanese people will feel secure about their way of life, their free-market system, and their hope for democracy.

Aggressive attempts to enter international organizations and gain diplomatic relations under a new but ambiguous name do not necessarily imply the emergence of an independent Taiwan state. If the PRC refrains from blackballing these attempts, or even tacitly agrees to them, the need for psychological security will be fulfilled in such a way that the advocacy for Taiwan independence will be deflated and the antagonism between Taiwan and China will be reduced, making a truly peaceful, friendly, and mutually beneficial relationship possible. Otherwise, tension will remain, the vast spending on arms and diplomatic battles will continue, and after repeated attempts foiled by the PRC, I predict the Taiwanese people will seek another way to break through with a much higher possibility that Taiwan would one day declare itself an independent state.

The Chairman (Harvey J. Feldman)
I wish to point out one essential fact because I have found in the past that some people don't understand this. To enter the United Nations, you need a recommendation from the Security Council to the General Assembly. And of course, as you all know, the PRC is a permanent member of the Security Council and therefore its negative vote on such a resolution would kill any application and it would never come to the General Assembly.

Hungdah Chiu
I will review the PRC's policies on the participation of the Republic of China on Taiwan, also called the Taiwan area, in international organizations.

After the establishment of the People's Republic of China on October 1, 1949, it adopted the one-China policy in its participation in international organizations, either governmental or nongovernmental. According to this policy, it will not tolerate the concurrent representation of the Republic of China on Taiwan in the same organization. But, as Professor Kau pointed out, before October 26, 1971, when the PRC took over the Chinese seat from the Republic of China at the UN, this policy backfired for the People's Republic of China. Before the Cultural Revolution in 1966, the Republic of China was represented in 39 intergovernmental organizations, while the PRC participated in only 1 international governmental organization. With respect to non-governmental international organizations, in 1966 the PRC participated in 58, and the ROC in 182.

The ROC's loss of the UN seat in 1971 significantly affected its participation in international organizations, especially intergovernmental organizations. Professor Kau said that there are about 10 intergovernmental organizations in which the ROC still maintains membership. His figure is based on the ROC Foreign Ministry's statistics. Actually the Permanent Court of International Arbitration already removed the Republic of China's name. The only thing it has not done is to send a notice of expulsion. In May 1990, another intergovernmental organization, the International Committee for Military Medicine and Pharmacy, also expelled the ROC when the PRC was admitted. So the situation is not very optimistic.

The PRC's policy before 1979 was to exclude the ROC on Taiwan from all international non-governmental and intergovernmental organizations. But the problem is, there are so many international non-governmental and intergovernmental organizations that it is simply not possible for the PRC to participate in all of them. So the ROC continued to increase its participation. If anyone is interested, there is a book called *The Yearbook of International Organizations* that also includes non-governmental organizations. I think there are at least two or three thousand non-governmental organizations listed there. The PRC before 1979 felt it could threaten to boycott international non-governmental organizations in order to make them not accept the participation of the ROC, especially in international sports activities affiliated with the International Olympic Committee. So in 1976 the ROC Olympic Team was forced to withdraw from the Montreal Olympics, and the PRC participated. But in 1979 the PRC changed its policy from liberation of Taiwan to peaceful unification, allowing Taiwan to retain its social and economic system after unification. In 1981 it changed its policy on the ROC's participation in international sports activities. On March 23, 1981, under an agreement with the International Olympic Committee, the Republic of China Olympic Committee changed its name to Chinese Taipei Olympic Committee and adopted a new flag because it was not allowed to use the national flag. It could then participate in all activities sponsored by the International Olympic Committee. From that point on, the problem of Taiwan's participation in international sports activities was basically solved.

This formula of "Chinese Taipei" or a similar one is also applicable to other international non-governmental organizations where the ROC and PRC are participating, and where the ROC is not allowed to use the term Republic of China. Since 1984 there have been at least 132 international non-governmental organizations where both the PRC and the ROC are members. The ROC has participated in those organizations under the name Chinese Taipei or something similar, but definitely not under the name Republic of China. However, if an international organization allows both governmental and private national organizations to be members, then the PRC will insist that it occupy the governmental seat. But it will not object to Taiwan occupying a non-governmental seat. For instance, the ROC was a governmental member of the International Institute of Administrative Sciences. In 1990, when the PRC was admitted as a governmental member, the ROC was expelled. Under the statutes of the Institute it can still join as a corporate member (non-governmental). Interestingly, the United States has also joined as a corporate member of the International Institute of Administrative Sciences and never joined as a governmental member. Using the formula of Chinese Taipei or a similar one, there should not be any serious problem for the ROC on Taiwan to participate in international non-governmental organizations in the 1990s.

On the question of international governmental organizations, the ROC is unable to join any such organization affiliated with the UN. In fact, it was expelled by all of those organizations after 1971. But in 1983 when the PRC indicated its intention to join the Asian Development Bank (ADB), it appeared that the PRC was willing to reconsider its policy of excluding Taiwan from all international governmental organizations. In July 1983 Deng Xiaoping told Professor Winston Yang of Seton Hall University that after admission of the PRC to the Asian Development Bank, Taiwan could retain its seat under the name Taipei China. In March 1986 the PRC was admitted into the ADB without expelling the ROC, but the ROC had to change its name to Taipei China. At that time, under the late President Chiang Ching-kuo, the ROC government protested the change of its name, but did not withdraw from the ADB. In May 1989, when the ADB had its annual meeting in Beijing, the ROC's new president, Lee Teng-hui, approved participation by a ministerial delegation, although still protesting the change of name.

Many in Taiwan hope that the ADB formula can be applied to Taiwan's participation in other international governmental organizations, so as to resolve one of the basic issues of unification. However, the PRC foreign ministry on December 19, 1988, rejected this and stated that it considers the ADB case a special exception not applicable to other international governmental organizations.

On the other hand, in 1984 the PRC also showed some flexibility on the question of Taiwan's representation in an intergovernmental organization to which the ROC already was a party. In that year, the PRC was admitted into the International Criminal Police Organization, but it did not demand the outright expulsion of the ROC delegation. It agreed Taiwan could have some form of representation, but without voting privileges because under the organization's charter, one country can have only one vote. Moreover, the ROC could not use the name ROC, but must change it to Taipei China or something similar. So the organization is still in the process of finding a satisfactory solution to keep Taiwan as a participant.

In 1989, as I mentioned earlier, when the PRC was admitted to the International Committee of Military Medicine and Pharmacy, the ROC was expelled. Therefore, the PRC's policy toward Taiwan's participation in international governmental organizations is not very consistent.

In early 1990 the ROC applied to join the General Agreement on Tariffs and Trade (GATT) under the name Taiwan, Penghu, Kinmen, Matsu Customs Territory, in accordance with Article 33 of the GATT. The PRC, which is an observer to GATT and is also applying for membership, opposes the ROC application for GATT membership, even though the ROC is willing to change its name. It stated, however, that after becoming a member, it would not object to Taiwan becoming a member in accordance with Article 24 of the agreement. In 1990, when the Asian Pacific Economic Cooperation Conference was discussing the question of admitting mainland China, Taiwan, and Hong Kong, the PRC expressed its objection to membership status for

Taiwan and Hong Kong, but agreed that they might have observer status. Is this an indication of a new PRC policy toward Taiwan's participation in international governmental organizations? It is not very clear.

Even if it is, we must ask whether Taiwan will be satisfied with such limited participation in international governmental organizations. The PRC's policy to exclude Taiwan from international governmental organizations is undercutting its attempt to win over people on Taiwan for the cause of unification. This is because many people on Taiwan feel that as long as Taiwan maintains its one-China policy and accepts the ultimate goal of unification, there's no reason to exclude their participation in international governmental organizations.

Many of the international governmental organizations in which Taiwan wishes to participate are non-political. They are useful, but not essential to Taiwan's economic and social development. This includes GATT, the International Civil Aviation Organization, the World Intellectual Property Organization, and many others. Many people on Taiwan feel that arrangements can be made under the Asian Development Bank formula approved by Deng Xiaoping, to avoid the two-China issue in which the PRC has a legitimate concern. However, it does not appear that the PRC is willing to adopt a new policy toward Taiwan's participation in international governmental organizations. They still hope, by isolating Taiwan from the international community, to force Taiwan to accept the One Country, Two Systems formula. Only after unification will the PRC allow Taiwan to have limited participation in international governmental organizations.

I think this is very unrealistic. While Taiwan's exclusion from many of these organizations may cause inconvenience for its international relations, trade, and foreign economic relations, it cannot deter the ROC on Taiwan from continued economic and trade development. Since 1971, while the ROC on Taiwan has been excluded from all major international governmental organizations, it has continued to prosper and develop. So the PRC leadership's refusal to adopt the ADB formula to resolve a major issue in Taiwan-mainland relations can only further alienate the Chinese people on Taiwan and make the prospect of peaceful unification even more remote.

David Dean
The PRC position on Taiwan has not been unchanging. Before 1979 it emphasized liberation, and after 1979, unification. In the Asian Development Bank the PRC changed its policy to allow Taiwan to have a separate status, separate voting rights, and separate membership. It is not impossible that, as time goes by, there will be other changes in the mainland's attitude toward Taiwan. Granted, the PRC will be looking after its own interests and its own long-term objectives, but I think the comments raised by Dr. Tsai Shih-yuan, and also by Professor Ying-mao Kau, suggest that the PRC has to be more sensitive and more constructive about its relationship with Taiwan if it doesn't want to drive Taiwan into actions that would make the situation even more difficult.

Let me talk a bit about Taiwan's change in its approach to international relations. I think that the ADB is a good starting point. I was involved tangentially in the negotiations that admitted the PRC and changed Taiwan's name in the bank. These negotiations went on in 1985-86. Taipei always took a very strong position that any change in its name in the ADB would affect its legitimacy and its sovereignty. These two points caused it to delay to the very last moment. Regardless of any proposal or counterproposal for the name change or for its position in the bank, it kept to the position that it would not change its name.

Yet the membership of the bank was very anxious to admit the PRC, and the PRC claimed it wouldn't come in if Taiwan retained the name Republic of China. All sorts of suggestions were made through the permanent staff of the ADB in Manila about various name changes that might be satisfactory to both sides. The PRC indicated which names it would accept. But Taiwan declined to indicate which names it might wish to accept until the very last moment. By the time it did indicate certain preferences, the die had already been cast for "Taipei China."

The reaction in Taiwan was that they would not send their delegation to the annual meeting of the ADB in the spring of 1986, and they boycotted it again in 1987. It wasn't until Lee Teng-hui assumed the presidency in early 1988 that a different decision was made. His news conference in February of 1988 reflected this change in attitude. I think he felt it was much more important to be present and to represent Taiwan's interests than to argue over the name. So he authorized the Taiwan delegation, led by the governor of the Central Bank, to go to Manila in the spring of 1988 to attend the annual meeting—a definite switch to a much more flexible approach to international relations. The delegation went, but put a sign on the desk saying "under protest," and they covered up the part of their name tag that said Taipei China. So they sort of made it into a protest meeting, which soured the feelings of everybody else present at the meeting because it overshadowed the fact that an agreement had been reached.

The following year, Shirley Kuo, the Finance Minister, led the Taiwan delegation to the ADB annual meeting in Beijing, the first government minister from Taiwan to attend an international meeting on the mainland in recent years. She conducted herself in such a dignified way that everyone including the hosts respected her and respected the presence of the delegation. When she got back home, however, she was criticized strongly by some elements because she, along with the rest of her delegation, had stood up like everyone else when the Chinese hosts came in, and had shaken hands with some of the hosts, instead of folding her hands and remaining seated. But most of the delegations in Beijing felt that she had acted in a very proper and civilized way, and that she had brought a great deal of credit on herself, her delegation, and Taiwan itself.

Then, in 1990 the delegation to the ADB went to New Delhi and there were no untoward incidents, no protests, or anything else. They acted as a normal delegation would act.

I think that the ADB decision forms a kind of watershed. Prior to that time, there was a very rigid feeling that any name change would be detrimental to Taiwan's interests, to its legitimacy, to its sovereignty, to its international position. However, after resuming its position in the ADB as a separate member with separate voting rights (although the PRC did say at that time that this was an unusual occurrence and was an exception) some people felt that it could turn into a precedent for membership in other international organizations. But that of course remains to be seen.

In any case, Taiwan's approach to international affairs at that point became much more flexible. The application for membership in GATT reflects that flexibility. Taiwan is applying as a customs territory, rather than as a national entity. The main problem is that the PRC has insisted it come into GATT first. There's always the possibility that perhaps they will want Taiwan to come in as a part of the PRC rather than as a separate entity, but that is not yet resolved.

I want to move now to changes in international perceptions about Taiwan. I think there are several factors that have caused other countries to become less sensitive to PRC concerns about their relations with Taiwan. In the first place, just the passage of time, almost twenty years since 1971 when the UN admitted the PRC in place of Taiwan, has blunted some of the PRC's pressures. Although Beijing has been consistent in objecting to any official relations between other countries and Taiwan, its oft-repeated complaints are gradually being taken for granted and they are less effective than they were twenty years ago.

Second, developments within mainland China have diminished its leverage on outsiders. The repercussions of the June 4 Tiananmen Incident, coupled with economic difficulties and an initial pullback on much needed economic and political reforms, have created the impression that mainland China will be preoccupied with its domestic troubles in the foreseeable future. As a result, Beijing's ability to influence others to act in accordance with its policies has diminished.

Third, the ending of the U.S./Soviet superpower rivalry has also weakened China's international role. It can no longer try to maneuver its relations with the U.S. and the Soviet Union to its own advantage.

Another important development is the relationship between Taiwan and the mainland. Since 1987 there has been a flood of travel from Taiwan to the mainland. There has been rapidly expanding trade. There have been substantial increases in Taiwan investment. There have been visits by members of the Legislative Yuan, academics, athletes, etc. This has had the effect of reducing tensions between Taiwan and the PRC. Other countries observing these developments feel more free to pursue their own economic and other substantive interests with Taiwan. Taiwan's policies, the abandonment of the Three Nos in favor of more positive policies, and calling for governmental talks under certain conditions have also captured the interest of other countries.

Still another factor is Taiwan's economic growth. Its status as the world's twelfth largest trading nation, its huge foreign exchange reserves, its substantial public and private investments in other countries, particularly in Southeast Asia but elsewhere too, including the United States, have attracted a great deal of attention. Taiwan's total trade last year was $118 billion. Taiwan is the United States' fifth largest trading partner. Other countries are seeking additional trade and investment from Taiwan, investment that is not available from the mainland. So the availability of capital makes Taiwan increasingly popular, especially with developing nations.

Another factor that has improved Taiwan's image and gained it more respect has been the political reforms carried out since 1987. These reforms are transforming Taiwan from an authoritarian government to a more democratic, popular government in a peaceful and reasonably orderly transition. This example is not lost on others.

All of these combined factors have helped Taiwan's substantive position. Other nations, judging from my own observations in Taipei, are taking a much closer look at what is happening there. In the last two or three years there have been large numbers of parliamentary delegations from France, England, Germany, and other places. I don't know how many U.S. Congressmen have traveled to Taiwan over the last few years, but certainly a large number. Businessmen too have come looking for some type of commercial, economic, or other contact. Many European countries have established trade offices, which are authorized now to issue visas. And they're staffing these trade offices with their foreign ministry personnel. It's much easier today for a traveler from Taiwan to get a visa to go to Europe than it was three years ago.

You can say it's all substantive, it's not official, and that's true. But it still creates a different type of atmosphere, and that coupled with the change in the atmosphere between Taiwan and the mainland means evolution in a direction that is probably going to be favorable to Taiwan. If I may make some predictions, I think Taiwan may well join GATT as a separate member, may well have some sort of observer status in other international financial organizations. I believe its annual statistics are being published in the World Bank Annual Report. Switzerland, which is not a member, has traditionally had its statistics published and I believe now Taiwan's are being published also. These are small things, but if you add them up, they represent a major change from ten years ago, even five years ago. In fact, the pace of these developments over the last three or four years has speeded up considerably.

I conclude with the thought that given the direction in which events are proceeding, provided that there is PRC concurrence which I understand is a necessary condition, we may well see greater representation in the international arena for Taiwan in the future.

—Floor Discussion—

Linda Gail Arrigo (Acting Director of Foreign Relations, DPP) I'd like to continue on the line of my colleague Tsai Shih-yuan, from the position of the DPP. Earlier this year, on behalf of the Taiwan democratic movement overseas, I proposed a series of projects for international contacts. Now, as acting foreign secretary of the DPP, I've also put together a series of projects. Of course, we don't have the financial capacity, the manpower resources of the ruling party. However, it seems that the ruling party will follow in our footsteps and magnify our efforts.

For example, at the United Nations, the Formosa Association for Public Affairs has recently kicked off an effort to make increasing contact with the United Nations. I don't expect that Taiwan is going to get membership soon, but it is encouraging that, judging from what I have heard from some observer missions, there is an increasing multilaterality within the United Nations. I expect that the independent efforts at breaking Taiwan's isolation will move in a multilateral direction, and the response is very encouraging. There is virtually no one who thinks that Taiwan is under the sovereignty of the PRC.

Our resources have to be put into many directions, especially since the Director of Foreign Relations for the DPP is being sent to jail for three and a half years. But, there is great interest among the Taiwanese overseas and also in Taiwan. When we invited some Hungarians from the opposition party to Taiwan, the Taiwan government discouraged their visas, but then jumped to invite a dozen itself, to which the PRC objected. Just before I left Taiwan, a delegation of legislators, including a number of DPP people, traveled through Eastern Europe and the Soviet Union.

I think that this is the age of sovereignty for small nations, and may it proceed.

The Chairman (Harvey J. Feldman)
Thank you. I was curious about not giving visas to Hungarians. The ROC has opened a trade office in Budapest and I thought it was encouraging contact.

Linda Arrigo
Yes, but they did not want the people we invited.

Thomas Stolper (author, *China, Taiwan, and the Offshore Islands*, 1985)
What was that about the Director of Foreign Relations for the DPP being sentenced to three years in jail?

Linda Arrigo
Li Tzung-fan, before he took over the position of Director of Foreign Relations, was the DPP candidate for County Executive of Tainan County. In the protest over vote counting, over what the opposition and the populace believed was ballot fraud, there was a riot at one of the court houses, and seven people were sentenced for a total of twenty years. Of course, we don't believe that there is any real justice involved here, it's just another attempt to stop the organization of the DPP.

The Chairman
I have a question I'd like to ask Ying-mao Kau. In listening to your presentation, I got a feeling that you think that flexible diplomacy is being stymied. Is this the impression that you meant to leave?

Ying-mao Kau
Diplomacy is an extension of internal politics. In internal politics we see a backlash of the conservatives, who tend to believe that dual recognition will lead to the possibility of two Chinas, or one China-one Taiwan, and that any enhancement of Taiwan's diplomatic status is going to increase Taiwan's international visibility and have some damaging effect on the traditional basis of the KMT's internal legitimacy. This is bound to stifle or frustrate the initiative of the Foreign Ministry.

My sense is that the president is quite frustrated, and particularly that the political crisis last spring was a miserable situation for him. Domestic sources of frustration were compounded by Beijing's attempt to encourage the conservatives in their opposition to diplomatic initiatives and the reform movement. I can sense his frustration, but I believe he is not likely to give up his vision. He wants to make Taiwan a technology power, exporting technology, not just shoes. With the new organization of the National Unification Commission perhaps he can take care of the conservative criticism for the time being.

Kuo Chen-lung (Reporter, *China Times*)
Domestic constraints are causing diplomacy to become less flexible. In that sense, the government's domestic autonomy and its diplomatic leverage are inversely related. If we put it in that perspective, we can see why Shirley Kuo was criticized when she came back from the ADB meeting in Beijing. But these pressures are not only from the conservatives. When the Americans want

to open up the Taiwan market, agricultural imports are opposed by a rising domestic agricultural pressure group. There is a conservative backlash, but it belongs in the same category as the agricultural import opposition and the small industries suffering from the rising value of Taiwan dollar.

The second thing I want to say is about the policy of *Han tsei pu liang-li*. Of course it has to do in part with KMT ideology. But I think it was also in close correspondence with the global containment policy of the United States. If you don't look at it from an international perspective, you are missing an important point.

The Chairman
I'd like to ask Ying-mao Kau to comment on the point that as the country democratizes, interest groups come to the fore. The farmers object to agricultural import liberalization, the conservatives and perhaps the military or others object to flexible diplomacy, and diplomacy becomes captive to the interest of various domestic groups.

Ying-mao Kau
It depends on which aspect of diplomacy you are talking about. It is true that certain interest groups try to protect their turkeys, or try to protect their ducks, and so on. But on the issue of the military, I think the picture is quite different. I think the military is confused. You've got Communist officials arriving in Chinmen for official negotiations. You say it's unofficial, but we know it's official. What are you going to tell the soldiers and the generals that they are defending against?

The military has made a confusing shift. In the past, the enemies were clearly defined as those across the Taiwan Straits. Now, according to the military, the enemy is internalized, it's the internal independence movement. So the military takes a cautious policy toward flexible diplomacy.

There is a logic in it, but the game is not really that simple. Internally, there is a surging demand for Taiwan's identity. Taiwan is a first-rate economic power, and the citizens do not want to be treated as second-rate citizens in the world. Unless you are a Taiwanese, you cannot fully appreciate that feeling. I don't know how to convey it. American citizens go everywhere and are treated royally.

Take a simple issue, the passport. A passport is a symbol of your national identity. When you go to Europe, a ROC passport gets you nowhere. I run into a friend on the plane and ask him, "Where are you going?" He says, "I'm going to Mexico to participate in a business deal, but I have been waiting in Taiwan for three months for a Mexican visa to be issued. My five million dollar deal is gone."

This psychological impact has been translated into domestic politics. The military and the conservative forces should not underestimate this mood of frustration in dealing with the issue of pragmatic diplomacy.

Hungdah Chiu
I think the situation is not as bad as Professor Kau believes. In the case of France, if you use a Republic of China passport, the visa will be issued in twenty-four hours. In both Germany and France, you can get multiple entry visas. The problem is in Third World countries like Mexico. I had an experience of that kind in Mexico in connection with an international meeting. They invited me to go, but refused to issue a visa. Finally they arranged for me to go to Mexico without a visa, and issued a piece of paper right at the airport. On the other hand, if you show a Chinese Communist passport to apply for a visa to France or Germany, it is more complicated and takes more time. They are all suspicious of the Communists.

The obstacles to flexible diplomacy are not so great inside Taiwan. I do not think there is any significant opposition to establishing diplomatic relations with more countries. The problem is that those countries, under heavy PRC pressure, are reluctant to establish diplomatic relations with the ROC. Take Equatorial Guinea, Trinidad and Tobago, and Madagascar as examples. They did negotiate with the ROC on establishment of diplomatic relations, but under heavy PRC pressure they backed out. It's not because someone in the ROC opposes President Lee's policy to establish diplomatic relations with more countries.

The Chairman
David Dean, is it true that *Han tsei pu liang-li* derives from U.S. policy?

David Dean
It is true that the United States supported the ROC as the sole legitimate government of China for many years. But the concept itself is not a U.S. concept, it's a Chinese concept. It's an internal policy of the authorities on Taiwan themselves. The U.S. in the Shanghai Communiqué acknowledged the Chinese position that Beijing is the sole legitimate government of China. From that point on through the Recognition Communiqué of January 1, 1979, to the August 17, 1982, Joint Communiqué, U.S. policy has gradually moved closer to the PRC position, not only on being the sole legitimate government, but also on the status of Taiwan.

Earlier, when we recognized Taipei, the official U.S. government position was that the status of Taiwan was undecided. That was the position held up until 1979.

Hungdah Chiu
In 1964, when France recognized the PRC, the United States urged the ROC's embassy to stay in Paris and not to break relations. But later the French government, under pressure from

the PRC, said to the ROC that they must leave or be expelled. There was already some flexibility at the time, but it did not work. On the other hand, in 1984 when Suriname wanted to establish diplomatic relations with the ROC, the ROC Foreign Minister at that time recommended to the late President Chiang Ching-kuo that he should require Suriname to sever diplomatic relations with the PRC first, before establishing diplomatic relations with the ROC, and the deal subsequently failed.

The issue also came up in regard to the ADB. At that time, many argued that the ADB is a bank, and government legitimacy is not tied to a bank. There were some conservative elements in Taiwan at that time strongly opposed to changing the ROC's name in order to stay in the ADB. I and many others wrote articles to oppose their position.

The Concluding Round Table: What If?

Andrew J. Nathan

We've heard that real power is in the hands of the parties. We've heard that real power is in the hands of the military. We've heard that real power is in the hands of the masses. So, who has power? How far will they push? How far will it go? Is it possible for reform to go to the extent that the DPP will actually take power? If the DPP actually takes power, what difference will it make? What policies will they change, if any? Will they change economic policy, environmental policy? Will they really change Taiwan's relations with the mainland?

On the question of society and social stability, we've heard two different views. One is that Taiwan is a very stable, middle-class place. There is an appearance of conflict, but the conflict is not really deep-going. People have their hands on one another's throats, but no one is really squeezing, and from time to time they wink at one another. Then we've heard that Taiwan is on the brink of an explosion. There is deep frustration. There is the possibility of various kinds of decay. Hau Pei-tsun may arrest people. The masses may rise up.

On the economic side we have also heard two very different views. One is the hollowing-out theory, that Taiwan is losing its manufacturing capabilities and will soon have nothing left to live on. And then there is the transition theory, that Taiwan is upgrading its manufacturing as well as becoming a service economy. Some people say that economic forces will push Taiwan and the mainland together because of their complementarity. But we've heard another view, that the economic maturation of Taiwan will bring Taiwan into greater integration with the advanced world economy and accelerate its separation from the mainland.

With regard to mainland-Taiwan political relations, one view is that the mainland is tightening the noose on Taiwan, and

Taiwan has fewer and fewer ways out and will eventually have to knuckle under. Another view is that Taiwan is strengthening its international viability in all kinds of ways, economically, politically, and diplomatically, so that eventually the mainland will be forced to change its policy.

We've heard it predicted that the stand-off between the two sides will go on indefinitely. Other people have said that there is a face-saving solution for both sides in which the mainland would accept the de facto independence of Taiwan, while the Taiwan residents would accept an independence which is merely de facto, if I can put it that way.

Here we have the people who are going to answer all these questions.

Antonio Chiang

I just came across a piece from today's newspaper. It said that if you have no nightmares, you are a person of no creativity and no imagination. On Taiwan people have a big nightmare; that's why we are so creative and imaginative. I also read a column some years ago that said that if Taiwan were a person it would be under psychiatric care. It has the world's most serious delusion of grandeur, claiming to be the government of China. Yet it is the ultimate realist too, doing business with everyone everywhere.

Chinese politics has a spirit of play. As a journalist working on the political development of Taiwan, I've come to see our politics as a kind of Chinese shadow boxing, *tai chi*. South Korean politics is a politics of confrontation, a politics of clubbing. But in Taiwan, there are all kinds of noise, all kinds of shadows, but you don't see any real action, no real confrontation, only gestures. It almost scares people to death, but they come out of it very smoothly. Throughout these years we have seen this kind of game played by the ruling party and the opposition. Their power struggles are a good example of Chinese or Taiwanese politics. The people who are against Lee Teng-hui did nothing, but Lee Teng-hui almost fell from his chair. Nobody did anything, nobody said anything, but our president almost lost his position.

Sometimes our politics is a kind of semantic game too. People are concerned about the rules, not necessarily about the substance. They are also careful in choosing their words. When they had the National Affairs Conference, they reached a conclusion, but now that conclusion is hotly disputed. Its conclusion concerning the election of our president is vague: it said popular election. It implies to some people, direct election. But it seems this is not necessarily so for the KMT. So the conclusion depends on how you define the term popular election.

Some people insist on saying Beiping, others say Beijing. Even now with more than two hundred journalists in Beijing, some say they are broadcasting from Beijing and others say from Beiping. When they say China, some say *Chung-hua* instead of *Chung-kuo*. They're always arguing about terms. Words mean much in politics in Taiwan.

The idea of *Han tsei pu liang-li* also reflects the mentality of Chinese political culture. In the past we said only one king on earth, only one heaven in the sky. So to allow the opposition to become a party is a painful and difficult breakthrough in Chinese tradition.

People like me, who view political development very closely because we have the privilege of sitting in the front row of the theater of politics, observe people like Yao Chia-wen and Chang Chün-hung who were in jail for so many years. So many people who suffered as political prisoners in the past. More than 10,000 went to jail. Once I attended the wedding ceremony of one of the former political prisoners. The master of ceremonies announced that there were more than 200 political prisoners among the guests of honor. Their total term on Green Island was more than 2000 years. That extends back before the birth of Christ.

So our political development has been a long process. But we have to take note that the Kuomintang is not so authoritarian, so dictatorial, so suppressive as other governments. Our KMT, I used to say, has no capacity for democracy, but also lacks the guts to be a real dictator. They keep changing the definition of "advocating independence," which is still a crime. Some years ago they said anybody advocating popular election or restructuring of parliament was advocating independence. And then they said that advocating self-determination is equivalent to advocating independence. Then they said that if you abolish martial law and have an opposition party, it's independence. When the opposition tried to establish the Public Policy Research Association, the KMT said that this was the equivalent of a party and had to be closed down. But the opposition fought on, established the Public Policy Association, and then wanted to establish branch offices. The KMT said, "You can keep your headquarters, but you can't set up branch offices." Still the opposition continued. Then, when the opposition organized itself as a party the KMT said, "You can keep your public policy association as long as you don't organize a party." When the DPP was set up they said, "You can have your party as long as you don't advocate independence." The retreat went on step by step. It became a democracy of events.

That kind of politics is a test of power. Sometimes it's easy for us to understand, but for foreigners it's hard to understand. Things don't change much in the way they are spoken of. We say one thing but do another. So in watching political developments, we should be very aware of subtle changes. For example, some people here have claimed to be reformers. Yes, every regime, even very authoritarian regimes, wants some kind of reform. It is easy to say that under Chiang Kai-shek and Chiang Ching-kuo we had an authoritarian regime, but now everything is democratized. It is easy to say, but if we had a timetable for further changes toward democracy, I do not believe everything would be changed according to that timetable. The timetable provided yesterday by Hong Yuh-Chin was a timetable for constitutional reform, but I don't believe in it because they say one thing but do another. There are all kinds of times set for when we have a national election, a presidential election, a KMT congress, and so on. These timetables are useful as a guide, but I think the problem in Taiwan's political development is that we don't trust the laws and regulations or the constitution. The problem we have to face now in Taiwan is not improving the functioning of the system, but structural change.

I think we have to change our structure in a way that can reflect Taiwan as a country. I don't really want to refer to the colonial rule of the KMT, but Taiwanese society is a kind of immigrant society. We have been separate from China for more than one hundred years. That's why it is difficult to establish a consensus on our national identity.

Yao Chia-wen

Many people say that if there were a DPP president, we would try to change the relationship between Taiwan and mainland China. They claim this is very dangerous, and could harm the security of Taiwan. The PRC might try to use force to attack Taiwan. But we in the DPP feel differently. We feel the actual status of Taiwan is that it is not part of China. As I said yesterday, when we describe the status quo of Taiwan, we have to acknowledge that the PRC does not have sovereignty over Taiwan, and Taiwan is not part of the PRC—just as we stated in a resolution two years ago. We based our statement on the San Francisco Peace Treaty of 1951. Since Japan did not return the sovereignty over Taiwan to China, neither to the PRC nor to the ROC, no one can say that the PRC has sovereignty over Taiwan, or that Taiwan is a part of the PRC. That was the purpose of our resolution two years ago. We tried to make it clear that to keep the Taiwan Straits situation unchanged means maintaining that Taiwan has independent sovereignty. This is a very important point. When people say to us we should not try to change the situation of Taiwan, we agree. Because to us this means doing nothing to change the independent sovereignty of Taiwan.

American policy in the Taiwan Relations Act says that the future of Taiwan, or the problem of the Taiwan Straits, should be decided by both sides. That means that without the agreement of Taiwan, Taiwan cannot become part of China. China cannot incorporate Taiwan by its own decision or act.

Two years ago, when I visited the Philippines, I had a talk with the late Senator Aquino's brother. He argued that he could not support Taiwan's separation from China because he did not want to see Mindanao separate from the Philippines. He went on to say that since the Philippines can maintain its relationship with Mindanao, why can't Taiwan maintain the relationship with China? I told him the situations are different because Mindanao is a part of the Philippines but Taiwan is not part of the PRC.

Many people, for example David Dean, have asked me to give a clear definition of what we mean by Taiwan independence. When Taiwanese talk about Taiwan independence, we do not say Taiwan wants to separate from China. We say we want to maintain the existing situation and not become part of China. Taiwan is not Quebec, Taiwan is not Puerto Rico, and Taiwan is not Mindanao. So we believe if Taiwan maintains its status quo, Taiwan will remain independent.

Please understand that the situation in Taiwan is not like the situation in Mongolia in 1945. At that time Mongolia got its independence with the acquiescence of the Nanking Government through the procedure of a plebescite. In Taiwan we do not need to go through such procedure just to maintain the present situation. Taiwan can be independent even without any declaration. This is the basic position of the DPP.

Edwin A. Winckler

Yesterday I discussed Taiwan's transition "from authoritarianism." Today, I turn to Taiwan's transition "to democracy." As yesterday, I will begin with some remarks about the state of discourse on this subject, then address the question of toward what kind of democracy Taiwan may be heading. After that I will explore three issues about Taiwan's transition "to democracy" raised by the comparative literature.

As regards discourse, I must note that this conference provides an unusual opportunity for scholars, diplomats, politicians, and other professions to talk to each other. Such diversity is all the more valuable given how little real constructive criticism, not to speak of mutual encouragement, academics give each other. This conference is the kind of dialogue that produces academic, as well as, perhaps, other kinds of progress. I should note that Harvey Feldman has long been one of the few people to command both diplomatic and academic discourse about Taiwan since he headed the Taiwan Desk in the late 1970s. I should also note that this panel includes Antonio Chiang, Taiwan's leading political journalist, one of the foremost shapers of discourse about Taiwan's transition. That Taiwan produces such shrewd commentary is itself a significant indicator, and accomplishment, of its political progress.

As regards the transition "to democracy" on Taiwan, a preliminary task is clarifying toward what kind of democracy Taiwan may be heading. I have addressed this issue in the conclusions to two published volumes. (Please see *Taiwan in a Time of Transition,* edited by Harvey Feldman and others, 1988; and *Democratization in Taiwan,* edited by Tun-jen Cheng and Stephan Haggard, 1991). There I argue that the main democratic alternatives for Taiwan are Japanese "fiduciary statism," American "interest pluralism," and continental European "consultative elitism." I suggest that Taiwan is starting its transition "to democracy" from close to the Japanese model, is much influenced by the American model, but may end up with a Chinese-Taiwanese adaptation of the continental European model as a compromise between the first two.

Today I must restrict myself to some more general issues that Western democracy poses for Taiwan. Everybody thinks he knows what democracy is, but everybody means something different by it. Democracy is not an absolute principle that always applies to everything. More democracy at one level may require less at another. Western scholars writing about Taiwan may not be so clear as they suppose about how democracy actually works in the West, not to mention how it may work on Taiwan. Even within the Western tradition, one can note three quite different conceptions of democracy.

A first concept is direct participatory democracy, the Periclean ideal for the elites of small ancient city-states, with some modern approximations in town hall or church-meeting democracy. I'm afraid this ideal sometimes gets translated into Chinese practice as "everybody has to agree, otherwise everybody can do what he wants." Such an anarchic concept of democracy will not much help Taiwan because, for example, organized party competition requires party discipline.

A second concept is indirect representational democracy, the Burckean ideal for mass participation in large modern nation-states. The preferred form has voters choosing between parties who present alternative platforms for future policies. This is what most people think happens regularly in Western countries. It seldom does. The last American presidential election was a notorious example: the important issues facing the United States were not addressed, and therefore voters did not have a clear choice. Recent comparative literature says that European party systems seldom give voters much policy influence either. Maybe Taiwan can achieve this ideal of programmatic party competition, but it should realize that nobody else is doing so.

What actually happens in the United States and Western Europe is a third kind of democracy that we might call "delayed defensive." The most that voters can do is to review the performance of the government after the fact, and throw the rascals out if necessary, particularly if they have violated procedural norms of the system. That's why scandals are so central. This form of democracy does not have programmatic parties. Instead it has constituency service and, except when malfeasance in office occurs, a high probability of reelection for incumbents. Japan too works this way, and Taiwan has been moving in that direction for some time. In evaluating KMT performance or assessing DPP alternatives, it is important to compare them to actual Western practice, not just Western or Chinese ideals.

As regards Taiwan's transition "to democracy," a first comparative issue concerns the roles that an existing constitution, even if previously inoperative, can perform during a transition. Juan Linz and Arend Lijphart, among others, have argued that the old constitution can facilitate democratization by reducing transaction costs, providing an important bridge from the old to the new system.

A first function is that the democratic provisions of the old constitution provide a basis for demanding liberalization and democratization. The 1947 Nationalist constitution, even while largely suspended, did play an important role as the legal basis for opposition demands that the KMT live up to it.

A second function the comparative literature says an existing constitution can perform during transition is to reassure people who need protection. For example, if an authoritarian minority is to step down, it requires assurances that the democratic majority will not later punish it. To facilitate the KMT's withdrawal, the DPP might consider leaving the KMT some of its constitutional advantages, or granting it some alternative ones, when revisions of the existing system are made. Some DPP leaders have already indicated they might be willing to do so, for example on the issue of retaining token mainland representation in new central representative organs.

A third function of an old constitution is to give institutional form to the new democracy. The 1947 Nationalist constitution contains some useful institutions (such as the National Assembly and the Legislative Yuan), some possibly useless ones (such as the Control and Examination Yuans), and some ambiguities (such as the issue of whether it is a presidential or parliamentary system). As Chiang Ching-kuo himself insisted, politicians willing, Taiwan could achieve full democracy within the framework of the existing constitution. I wish Taiwan would do that. Otherwise, arguing about a new document will waste time and polarize politics when centrists could have been struggling for concrete measures that would actually implement democracy.

A long-discussed issue about the Nationalist constitution is whether it prescribes a presidential or parliamentary system. It contains elements of both, either of which could be emphasized. Juan Linz has suggested that the winner-take-all nature of presidential contests does not facilitate transition as well as the incrementally divisible nature of parliamentary elections. Presidentialism raises the intensity of political conflict and increases the possibility that losing parties will repudiate the system. On Taiwan, the DPP favors presidentialism because it might win a one-on-one presidential contest sooner than it might win a majority in parliament. Again, one hopes that the DPP will balance its short-run interests against its long-run interests.

A second comparative issue about the transition to democracy goes beyond narrowly constitutional issues to a broadly political question: who is going to win, the KMT or the DPP?

In the short run the KMT is a formidable antagonist with strong connections to many sectors of society. One does not expect it to roll over and play dead any time soon. That is why my timetable for transition would be gradual.

In the middle run one expects a standoff between the KMT and DPP. That alarms some people because it implies that no one will be clearly in charge. However, Dankwart Rustow argued in 1970 that it is from just such a stalemate that new democratic rules of the game will emerge. Only when each side finds that it can't get rid of the other will they be willing to agree on rules by which they can live with each other. One cannot, as Nationalist conservatives sometimes argue, fully establish the rules first, and only then play the game.

For the long run, recent comparative literature has a counter-intuitive implication for Taiwan. Most people would think that, starting from a one-party-dominant authoritarianism, one would be likely to end up with a one-party-dominant democracy. However, the historical record suggests otherwise. First, continued dominance by a previously authoritarian party of the right is infrequent, even when that party correctly expresses the nationalistic sentiments of the public. Second, the eventual emergence of another dominant party is less frequent than continued competition or stalemate. Third, in the few cases where a successor dominant party has emerged, usually it has been a party of the left that has responded to the socioeconomic demands unleashed by democratization. For Taiwan this could mean that long-run prospects for the DPP are quite bright, since the DPP, not the KMT, expresses Taiwanese nationalism, and the DPP claims to be socioeconomically progressive. On the other hand, the KMT could realign itself with Taiwanese nationalism, and is already fielding socioeconomic programs.

A third and last comparative issue goes beyond political issues to socioeconomic ones: What kind of policies will the new democracy adopt? Guillermo O'Donnell and Philippe Schmitter posit an "economic moment" as part of the completion of transition. The aspiration of the age is some kind of social democracy guaranteeing people economic and social, as well as political rights. This requires that the DPP move on from preoccupation with constitutional-political issues to formulate credible social programs.

Under the social democratic "moment," the first question is what to do about old deals? In the past there have been many special arrangements made and some people are already getting social benefits, mostly state employees, particularly mainlanders. Some of these benefits probably should stop, mainly those for privileged institutions, such as KMT economic monopolies. Other benefits probably should continue, mainly those for disadvantaged individuals, such as pensions for retired servicemen.

Second is the question of new deals, particularly how the KMT and DPP will come to terms with Taiwan's capitalist class. Arguably the biggest threat to the KMT is not the DPP, but businessmen. It wouldn't surprise me if sometime after the year 2000 the famous autonomy of the Nationalist state dissolved in a pool of money. In any case, it will be important on what terms, and with what objectives, business is brought into Taiwan's future democracy.

A third question about the socioeconomic stage of transition is the New Deal between capitalist owners and capitalist workers. What kind of social-democratic arrangements will be made for the public at large? This question suggests the need for long conversations between academics, professionals, and politicians about what the realistic alternatives are for social policies on Taiwan.

Yesterday I began by saying that the general theme I would address both yesterday and today is the question: Is Taiwan's political miracle half full or half empty? Yesterday I stressed the half-empty side. Today I want to conclude on a more upbeat note. I am optimistic about the long-range future of democracy, and a lot of other things, on Taiwan. The glass really is at least half full, and getting fuller. In fact, the real Taiwan political miracle may turn out to be that, even though it cannot physically recapture the mainland, by the early twenty-first century Taiwan will have captured the political imagination of many people on the mainland. To some extent it already has. However, this will continue only if all the parties involved take a broad view of who they are as Taiwanese, as Chinese, and as members of the global community. I hope this conference may have been one happy instance of Taiwan's participation in that global community.

—Floor Discussion—

Catherine Farris (Post-Doctoral Research Scholar, East Asian Institute, Columbia University)
On the schedule that you gave us, this concluding round table was supposed to include a discussion of insights gathered or omitted during the conference. One of the main things that has been omitted is the role of women in the political process. Richard Solomon once wrote a book on the political culture in Chinese society for which he interviewed male Chinese in Hong Kong. He decided not to interview any women because he argued that women traditionally played no role in the political process in Chinese society.

The presence at this conference of all male panelists, with the sole exception of Linda Arrigo, I think underscores the tacit assumption that politics, especially in China, is a male domain in which women have no place. Shirley Kuo has been mentioned several times, and I think she is one of the few women politicians in Taiwan of national stature. And she's clearly a token. There has also been mention of rising social activism in Taiwan. We've seen that women's groups have been participating in social activism on environmental issues, consumer issues, protesting child prostitution, employment practices, and so on. Clearly, women in Taiwan are interested in mobilizing and actively taking part in the political process.

My question is for any of the panelists, but especially our Chinese colleagues. Do you think political parties in Taiwan will encourage political participation by women in the political process? Will the major political parties actively support women for elected offices? Will there be efforts made to reform unfair divorce laws and child custody laws? Will there be enforcement of the equal inheritance laws that are already on the books? Should there be a move toward general equality as part of the process of democratization in Taiwan?

Antonio Chiang

Some years ago, when most of the opposition leaders were in jail, many of their wives became actively involved in politics. At that time we had a joke saying that the most effective way to promote the women's movement is to erase the husbands. All their potential sovereignty at that point will come into full force. I think this is a very good test for how much potential they have. I'm not in the best position to talk about women's role in Taiwan's politics. But as someone from Taiwan, I can assure you that we have a great flood of women journalists, including editors as well as reporters. About half of the staff in my office is female. In terms of politics, there are many able female politicians, like my friend Yao Chia-wen's wife who is the magistrate of Changhua. There are others as well. Women's political status in Taiwan is probably the best in Asia. Some of the movements headed by women are much more radical than those headed by men. They account for all kinds of activities and publications.

In the social and cultural sense, the movement does encounter very serious obstacles. There are people in the movement who feel very frustrated. But the movement always comes together and goes forward.

Yao Chia-wen

My wife was elected as the magistrate in our home county. Many people, especially those in the KMT, cannot accept the fact that Changhua County should be ruled by a woman. So she's faced a lot of problems.

In Taiwan, women need training to be active in politics. Political activities are hard and need a lot of knowledge and experience. Most women don't want to be politicians because this is a very hard job. This is so even though the KMT constitution is not unfair to women. I think this is a question of culture and tradition.

Michael Wei (Associate Professor, Graduate Institute of Social Welfare, National Chung-Cheng University)
Mr. Chiang comments that there have been a lot of changes in KMT policies during the past ten or so years, but Mr. Chiang sees this as the retreat of the KMT. Mr. Yao Chia-wen also mentioned that America's China policy is unclear and changing. It used to be the "one-China-but-not-now" policy and then it became something else. Why do policies change?

David Easton taught us that changes in policy follow the actors' interactions and changes in environments and ideology. Maybe this is the reason why the KMT made changes. I don't know whether this is also the reason for changes in American policy, but from my point of view as a KMT member, I think the answer is flexibility.

I admire and respect our friends from the DPP, but it is very easy to criticize the ruling party from a micro point of view. I will respect you more if you can take a macro point of view. That would make your judgments more reasonable.

Index

Studies of the East Asian Institute
Columbia University

The East Asian Institute is Columbia University's center for research, publication, and teaching on modern East Asia. The Studies of the East Asian Institute were inaugurated in 1962 to bring to a wider public the results of significant new research on modern and contemporary East Asia.

This book was supported by the Taiwan Area Studies Program, which is supported by a grant to the East Asian Institute from the Institute of International Relations, National Chengchi University.

STUDIES OF THE EAST ASIAN INSTITUTE

The Ladder of Success in Imperial China, by Ping-ti Ho. New York: Columbia University Press, 1962.

The Chinese Inflation, 1937–1949, by Shun-hsin Chou. New York: Columbia University Press, 1963.

Reformer in Modern China: Chang Chien, 1853–1926, by Samuel Chu. New York: Columbia University Press, 1965.

Research in Japanese Sources: A Guide, by Herschel Webb with the assistance of Marleigh Ryan. New York: Columbia University Press, 1965.

Society and Education in Japan, by Herbert Passin. New York: Teachers College Press, 1965.

Agricultural Production and Economic Development in Japan, 1873–1922, by James I. Nakamura. Princeton: Princeton University Press, 1967.

Japan's First Modern Novel: Ukigumo of Futabatei Shimel, by Marleigh Ryan. New York: Columbia University Press, 1967.

The Korean Communist Movement, 1918–1948, by Dae-Sook Suh. Princeton: Princeton University Press, 1967.

The First Vietnam Crisis, by Melvin Gurtov. New York: Columbia University Press, 1967.

Cadres, Bureaucracy, and Political Power in Communist China, by A. Doak Barnett. New York: Columbia University Press, 1968.

The Japanese Imperial Institution in the Tokugawa Period, by Herschel Webb. New York: Columbia University Press, 1968.

Higher Education and Business Recruitment in Japan, by Koya Azumi. New York: Teachers College Press, 1969.

The Communists and Peasant Rebellions: A Study in the Rewriting of Chinese History, by James P. Harrison, Jr. New York: Atheneum, 1969.

How the Conservatives Rule Japan, by Nathaniel B. Thayer. Princeton: Princeton University Press, 1969.

Aspects of Chinese Education, edited by C.T. Hu. New York: Teachers College Press, 1970.

Documents of Korean Communism, 1918–1948, by Dae-Sook Suh. Princeton: Princeton University Press, 1970.

Japanese Education: A Bibliography of Materials in the English Language, by Herbert Passin. New York: Teachers College Press, 1970.

Economic Development and the Labor Market in Japan, by Koji Taira. New York: Columbia University Press, 1970.

The Japanese Oligarchy and the Russo-Japanese War, by Shumpei Okamoto. New York: Columbia University Press, 1970.

Imperial Restoration in Medieval Japan, by H. Paul Varley. New York: Columbia University Press, 1971.

Japan's Postwar Defense Policy, 1947–1968, by Martin E. Weinstein. New York: Columbia University Press, 1971.

Election Campaigning Japanese Style, by Gerald L. Curtis. New York: Columbia University Press, 1971.

China and Russia: The "Great Game," by O. Edmund Clubb. New York: Columbia University Press, 1971.

Money and Monetary Policy in Communist China, by Katharine Huang Hsiao. New York: Columbia University Press, 1971.

The District Magistrate in Late Imperial China, by John R. Watt. New York: Columbia University Press, 1972.

Law and Policy in China's Foreign Relations: A Study of Attitude and Practice, by James C. Hsiung. New York: Columbia University Press, 1972.

Pearl Harbor as History: Japanese-American Relations, 1931–1941, edited by Dorothy Borg and Shumpei Okamoto, with the assistance of Dale K. A. Finlayson. New York: Columbia University Press, 1973.

Japanese Culture: A Short History, by H. Paul Varley. New York: Praeger, 1973.

Doctors in Politics: The Political Life of the Japan Medical Association, by William E. Steslicke. New York: Praeger, 1973.

The Japan Teachers Union: A Radical Interest Group in Japanese Politics, by Donald Ray Thurston. Princeton: Princeton University Press, 1973.

Japan's Foreign Policy, 1868–1941: A Research Guide, edited by James William Morley. New York: Columbia University Press, 1974.

Palace and Politics in Prewar Japan, by David Anson Titus. New York: Columbia University Press, 1974.

The Idea of China: Essays in Geographic Myth and Theory, by Andrew March. Devon, England: David and Charles, 1974.

Origins of the Cultural Revolution, by Roderick MacFarquhar. New York: Columbia University Press, 1974.

Shiba Khan: Artist, Innovator, and Pioneer in the Westernization of Japan, by Calvin L. French. Tokyo: Weatherhill, 1974.

Insei: Abdicated Sovereigns in the Politics of Late Heian Japan, by G. Cameron Hurst. New York: Columbia University Press, 1975.

Embassy at War, by Harold Joyce Noble. Edited with an introduction by Frank Baldwin, Jr. Seattle: University of Washington Press, 1975.

Rebels and Bureaucrats: China's December 9ers, by John Israel and Donald W. Klein. Berkeley: University of California Press, 1975.

Deterrent Diplomacy, edited by James William Morley. New York: Columbia University Press, 1976.

House United, House Divided: The Chinese Family in Taiwan, by Myron L. Cohen. New York: Columbia University Press, 1976.

Escape from Predicament: Neo-Confucianism and China's Evolving Political Culture, by Thomas A. Metzger. New York: Columbia University Press, 1976.

Cadres, Commanders, and Commissars: The Training of the Chinese Communist Leadership, 1920–45, by Jane L. Price. Boulder, CO: Westview Press, 1976.

Sun Yat-sen: Frustrated Patriot, by C. Martin Wilbur. New York: Columbia University Press, 1977.

Japanese International Negotiating Style, by Michael Blaker. New York: Columbia University Press, 1977.

Contemporary Japanese Budget Politics, by John Creighton Campbell. Berkeley: University of California Press, 1977.

The Medieval Chinese Oligarchy, by David Johnson. Boulder, CO: Westview Press, 1977.

The Arms of Kiangnan: Modernization in the Chinese Ordnance Industry, 1860-1895, by Thomas L. Kennedy. Boulder, CO: Westview Press, 1978.

Patterns of Japanese Policymaking: Experiences from Higher Education, by T. J. Pempel. Boulder, CO: Westview Press, 1978.

The Chinese Connection: Roger S. Greene, Thomas W. Lamont, George E. Sokolsky, and American-East Asian Relations, by Warren I. Cohen. New York: Columbia University Press, 1978.

Militarism in Modern China: The Career of Wu P'ei-fu, 1916-1939, by Odoric Y. K. Wou. Folkestone, England: Dawson, 1978.

A Chinese Pioneer Family: The Lins of Wu-Feng, by Johanna Meskill. Princeton University Press, 1979.

Perspectives on a Changing China, edited by Joshua A. Fogel and William T. Rowe. Boulder, CO: Westview Press, 1979.

The Memoirs of Li Tsung-jen, by T.K. Tong and Li Tsung-jen. Boulder, CO: Westview Press, 1979.

Unwelcome Muse: Chinese Literature in Shanghai and Peking, 1937-1945, by Edward Gunn. New York: Columbia University Press, 1979.

Yenan and the Great Powers: The Origins of Chinese Communist Foriegn Policy, by James Reardon-Anderson. New York: Columbia University Press, 1980.

Uncertain Years: Chinese-American Relations, 1947-1950, edited by Dorothy Borg and Waldo Heinrichs. New York: Columbia University Press, 1980.

The Fateful Choice: Japan's Advance into Southeast Asia, edited by James William Morley. New York: Columbia University Press, 1980.

Tanaka Giichi and Japan's China Policy, by William F. Morton. Folkestone, England: Dawson, 1980; New York: St. Martin's Press, 1980.

The Origins of the Korean War: Liberation and the Emergence of Separate Regimes, 1945–1947, by Bruce Cumings. Princeton: Princeton University Press, 1981.

Class Conflict in Chinese Socialism, by Richard Curt Kraus. New York: Columbia University Press, 1981.

Education Under Mao: Class and Competition in Canton Schools, by Jonathan Unger. New York: Columbia University Press, 1982.

Private Academies of Tokugawa Japan, by Richard Rubinger. Princeton: Princeton University Press, 1982.

Japan and the San Francisco Peace Settlement, by Michael M. Yoshitsu. New York: Columbia University Press, 1982.

New Frontiers in American-East Asian Relations: Essays Presented to Dorothy Borg, edited by Warren I. Cohen. New York: Columbia University Press, 1983.

The Origins of the Cultural Revolution: II, The Great Leap Forward, 1958–1960, by Roderick MacFarquhar. New York: Columbia University Press, 1983.

The China Quagmire: Japan's Expansion of the Asian Continent, 1933–1941, edited by James William Morley. New York: Columbia University Press, 1983.

Fragments of Rainbows: The Life and Poetry of Saito Mokichi, 1882–1953, by Amy Vladeck Heinrich. New York: Columbia University Press, 1983.

The U.S.–South Korean Alliance: Evolving Patterns of Security Relations, edited by Gerald L. Curtis and Sung-joo Han. Lexington, MA: Lexington Books, 1983.

Discovering History in China; American Historical Writing on the Recent Chinese Past, by Paul A. Cohen. New York: Columbia University Press, 1984.

The Foreign Policy of the Republic of Korea, edited by Youngnok Koo and Sungjoo Han. New York: Columbia University Press, 1984.

State and Diplomacy in Early Modern Japan, by Ronald Toby. Princeton: Princeton University Press, 1983 (hc); Stanford: Stanford University Press, 1991 (pb).

Japan and the Asian Development Bank, by Dennis Yasutomo. New York: Praeger Publishers, 1983.

Japan Erupts: The London Naval Conference and the Manchurian Incident, edited by James W. Morley. New York: Columbia University Press, 1984.

Japanese Culture, third edition, revised, by Paul Varley. Honolulu: University of Hawaii Press, 1984.

Japan's Modern Myths: Ideology in the Late Meiji Period, by Carol Gluck. Princeton: Princeton University Press, 1985.

Shamans, Housewives, and other Restless Spirits: Women in Korean Ritual Life, by Laurel Kendell. Honolulu: University of Hawaii Press, 1985.

Human Rights in Contemporary China, by R. Randle Edwards, Louis Henkin, and Andrew J. Nathan. New York: Columbia University Press, 1986.

The Pacific Basin: New Challenges for the United States, edited by James W. Morley. New York: Academy of Political Science, 1986.

The Manner of Giving: Strategic Aid and Japanese Foreign Policy, by Dennis T. Yasutomo. Lexington, MA: Lexington Books, 1986.

Security Interdependence in the Asia Pacific Region, James W. Morley, ed. Lexington, MA: D.C. Heath and Co., 1986.

China's Political Economy: The Quest for Development since 1949, by Carl Riskin. Oxford: Oxford University Press, 1987.

Anvil of Victory: The Communist Revolution in Manchuria, by Steven I. Levine. New York: Columbia University Press, 1987.

Urban Japanese Housewives: At Home and in the Community, by Anne E. Imamura. Honolulu: University of Hawaii Press, 1987.

China's Satellite Parties, by James D. Seymour. Armonk, NY: M.E. Sharpe, 1987.

The Japanese Way of Politics, by Gerald L. Curtis. New York: Columbia University Press, 1988.

Border Crossings: Studies in International History, by Christopher Thorne. Oxford & New York: Basil Blackwell, 1988.

The Indochina Tangle: China's Vietnam Policy, 1975–1979, by Robert S. Ross. New York: Columbia University Press, 1988.

Remaking Japan: The American Occupation as New Deal, by Theodore Cohen, edited by Herbert Passin. New York: The Free Press, 1987.

Kim Il Sung: The North Korean Leader, by Dae-Sook Suh. New York: Columbia University Press, 1988.

Japan and the World, 1853–1952: A Bibliographic Guide to Recent Scholarship in Japanese Foreign Relations, by Sadao Asada. New York: Columbia University Press, 1988.

Contending Approaches to the Political Economy of Taiwan, edited by Edwin A. Winckler and Susan Greenhalgh. Armonk, NY: M.E. Sharpe, 1988.

Aftermath of War: Americans and the Remaking of Japan, 1945–1952, by Howard B. Schonberger. Kent, OH: Kent State University Press, 1989.

Single Sparks: China's Rural Revolutions, edited by Kathleen Hartford and Steven M. Goldstein. Armonk, NY: M.E. Sharpe, 1989.

Neighborhood Tokyo, by Theodore C. Bestor. Stanford: Stanford University Press, 1989.

Missionaries of the Revolution: Soviet Advisers and Chinese Nationalism, by C. Martin Wilbur Julie Lien-ying How. Cambridge, MA: Harvard University Press, 1989.

Education in Japan, by Richard Rubinger and Edward Beauchamp. Honolulu: University of Hawaii Press, 1989.

Financial Politics in Contemporary Japan, by Frances Rosenbluth. Ithaca: Cornell University Press, 1989.

Suicidal Narrative in Modern Japan: The Case of Dazai Osamu, by Alan Wolfe. Princeton: Princeton University Press, 1990.

Thailand and the United States: Development, Security and Foreign Aid, by Robert Muscat. New York: Columbia University Press, 1990.

State Power, Finance and Industrialization of Korea, by Jung-Eun Woo. New York: Columbia University Press, 1990.

Anarchism and Chinese Political Culture, by Peter Zarrow. New York: Columbia University Press, 1990.

Competitive Ties: Subcontracting in the Japanese Automotive Industry, by Michael Smitka. New York: Columbia University Press, 1990.

China's Crisis: Dilemmas of Reform and Prospects for Democracy, by Andrew J. Nathan. Columbia University Press, 1990.

The Study of Change: Chemistry in China, 1840-1949, by James Reardon-Anderson. New York: Cambridge University Press, 1991.

Explaining Economic Policy Failure: Japan and the 1969-1971 International Monetary Crisis, by Robert Angel. New York: Columbia University Press, 1991.

Pacific Basin Industries in Distress: Structural Adjustment and Trade Policy in the Nine Industrialized Economies, edited by Hugh T. Patrick with Larry Meissner. New York: Columbia University Press, 1991.

From Bureaucratic Polity to Liberal Corporatism: Business Associations and the New Political Economy of Thailand, by Anek Laothamatas. Boulder, CO: Westview Press, 1991.

Constitutional Reform and the Future of the Republic of China, edited by Harvey J. Feldman. Armonk, NY: M.E. Sharpe, 1991.

Asia for the Asians: Japanese Advisors, Chinese Students, and the Quest for Modernization, 1895-1905, by Paula S. Harrell. Stanford: Stanford University Press, forthcoming.

The Political Impact of Economic Growth in the Asia-Pacific Region: The Experience of Nine Countries, edited by James W. Morley. Armonk, NY: M. E. Sharpe, forthcoming.

Locality and State: Schoolhouse Politics During the Chinese Republic, by Helen Chauncey. Princeton: Princeton University Press, forthcoming.